THE FOUR-FOLD WAY

Books of Similar Interest from Harper San Francisco

THE FOUR-FOLD WAY

Walking the Paths of the Warrior, Teacher, Healer, and Visionary

Angeles Arrien, Ph.D.

HarperSanFrancisco

A Division of HarperCollinsPublishers

HarperSanFrancisco and the author, in association with the Rainforest Action Network, will facilitate the planting of two trees for every one tree used in the manufacture of this book.

For information about workshops on the Four-Fold Way training programs contact:
    Office of Angeles Arrien
    P. O. Box 2077
    Sausalito, CA 94966

Design and Production: TBH/Typecast, Cotati

FIRST EDITION

Library of Congress Cataloging-in-Publication Data

Arrien, Angeles.
    The four-fold way : walking the paths of the warrior, teacher, healer, and visionary / Angeles Arrien. — 1st ed.
      p.   cm.
    Includes bibliographical references and index.
    ISBN 0-06-250059-7 (alk. paper)
  1. Shamanism.   2. Archetype (Psychology)   3. Interpersonal relations.   I. Title.
    BF1611.A76 1992
    291—dc20   91-55334
                                                               CIP

02 03 04 05 RRD H   23 24 25 26 27 28 29 30

Make prayers to the Raven.
Raven that is,
Raven that was,
Raven that always will be.
Make prayers to the Raven.
Raven, bring us luck.
—from the Koyukon, *Ravensong*

For my father,
Salvador Arrien,

whose pioneering spirit brought him from
the Pyrenees of Spain to the valleys of Idaho.
His deep connection to nature as a sheepherder
for over twenty years instilled in him a quiet
self-containment and an unquestionable strength
of character. He was a respected man whose
strong presence and unshakable integrity inspired
excellence.

CONTENTS

Acknowledgments xiii

Declaration xvii

Introduction 1

The Way of the Warrior 13

Showing Up and Choosing to Be Present 15

Empowerment Tools of the Warrior 25

The Warrior's Connection to Nature 29

How the Unclaimed Warrior/Leader Reveals
  Itself: The Shadow Aspects of the Warrior
  Archetype, the Wounded Child of the North 33

Processes and Reminders: Important Practices
  to Develop the Inner Warrior 37

Summary of the Warrior Archetype 40

The Way of the Healer 47

Pay Attention to What Has Heart and Meaning 49

Empowerment Tools of the Healer 54

The Healer's Connection to Nature 62

How the Unclaimed Healer Reveals Itself:
  The Shadow Aspects of the Healer
  Archetype, the Wounded Child of the South 65

Processes and Reminders: Important Practices
  to Develop the Inner Healer 69

Summary of the Healer Archetype 74

The Way of the Visionary 77

Tell the Truth without Blame or Judgment 79

Empowerment Tools of the Visionary 85

The Visionary's Connection to Nature 92

How the Unclaimed Visionary Reveals
    Itself: The Shadow Aspects of the Visionary
    Archetype, the Wounded Child of the East 93

Processes and Reminders: Important Practices
    to Develop the Inner Visionary 100

Summary of the Visionary Archetype 103

The Way of the Teacher 107

Be Open to Outcome, not Attached to Outcome 109

Empowerment Tools of the Teacher 116

The Teacher's Connection to Nature 119

How the Unclaimed Teacher Reveals Itself:
    The Shadow Aspects of the Teacher
    Archetype, the Wounded Child of the West 120

Processes and Reminders: Important Practices
    to Develop the Inner Teacher 123

Summary of the Teacher Archetype 126

Conclusion 129

Appendices 135

Appendix A: Eleanor Roosevelt's International Bill
  of Human Rights   137

Appendix B: World Council of Indigenous Peoples:
  Declaration of Principles   147

Appendix C: Haudenosaunee, or Six Nations Iroquois
  Confederacy, Statement to the World—May 1979   151

Appendix D: The Use of "Native American"   157

Appendix E: The Journey of the Drum   159

Listing of Graphics   173

Copyright Acknowledgments   177

Bibliography   181

Index   195

ACKNOWLEDGMENTS

I am grateful to my ancestors and family for providing me with such a rich heritage. Through their contributions and pioneering Basque spirit, they have inspired me to stay connected with Nature and to bridge an ancient origin with contemporary times. Because of this influence, my Four-Fold Way trainings have been designed to honor the perennial wisdoms found among the indigenous peoples of each continent so that the legacies of land-based peoples are not lost and are retained to further attend to the husbandry and stewardship of Mother Earth.

Many have come forward to support the Four-Fold Way training programs and this book. To those people and organizations who have supported the trainings to take place in natural environments, I am deeply thankful: Bob Mosby and Jo Norris of The Rim Institute and Brugh Joy, M.D., at Moonfire Lodge in Arizona; Nancee and Hugh Redmond at the Transformational Arts Institute in Redlands, California; Sylvia Lafair and Herb Kaufman at Creative Energy Options in Philadelphia, Pennsylvania; Fritz and Vivienne Hull and Elizabeth Campbell at Chinook Learning Center, Whidbey Island, Washington; Susan Osborn, David Densmore, and Donna Laslo of Songhouse Productions, Eastsound, Washington; Kit Wilson and Greta Holmes in Phoenix, Arizona; Dwight Judy and Bob Schmitt at the Institute of Transpersonal Psychology; the communities of Mount Madonna Center and Esalen Institute in the Monterey Bay area; and professional colleagues and friends who have supported and inspired my work, especially Christina and Stan Grof, Frances Vaughan and Roger Walsh,

Frank Lawlis and Jeanne Achterberg, Brooke Medicine Eagle, Leslie Gray, Luisah Teisch, and Michael Harner.

To all my students who have participated in the Four-Fold Way training, my graduate students and colleagues at the California Institute of Integral Studies, San Francisco, California, and the Institute of Transpersonal Psychology, Palo Alto, California, I am constantly enriched by the teachings extended to me in our learning and growing together. I am especially grateful to Phyllis Green for her persistence in establishing the first pilot group for the Four-Fold Way, and to Jim Dincalci for synthesizing the notes and material from my Cross-Cultural Healing classes which established the basic structure for the training.

I would have not been able to do the trainings without the help of Twainhart Hill and Carolyn Cappai. Their excellent administrative skills, support, and quality input for four and a half years of commitment to supervising all the logistics connected with the training program and my basic office operations made this all possible. Nancy Feehan and Kim Cottingham have been the base camp crew for all the solo wilderness programs connected with the year-long trainings. In addition, Nancy scouts the land and acreages for these experiences, and Kim functions as the gourmet base camp cook. The residential training programs have been logistically supported by Jane McKean, and assisted on site by the quality of work, consultation, and contribution of the drumming and anchor team comprised at different times by Mo Maxfield, June Steiner, Peter Lyon, Judy Ostrow, Nancy Feehan, and Paul Hinckley.

This book addresses some of the basic principles found in the Four-Fold Way training. I am deeply grateful to my literary lawyer Brad Bunnin, and my editor at Harper San Francisco, Mark Salzwedel. These gentlemen recognized and supported the vision of this book. To the other committed staff at Harper who supported actualizing this book in their own ways, I extend heartfelt appreciation to Michael Toms, Dean Burrell, Jeff

Campbell, Jamie Sue Brooks, Adrian Morgan, Naomi Lucks, Robin Seaman, Judith Beck, and Bill Turner.

In the initial stages of writing this book, I was supported by Kathy Altman who helped me see the possibilities connected with the work. I was additionally blessed with the patience and diverse skills of Diane Smith who spent concentrated transcribing and computer hours entering the material for me. Connie King and her excellent sense of design helped me select and integrate examples of cave art found around the world. She graphically rendered and synthesized the material found within the circular charts in each chapter. Twainhart Hill was responsible for bringing together the multiple details associated with the preparation of this material. She and Rosalyn Miller spent many hours tracking the permissions.

I respect the first and second generations of the ethnic peoples of the world for they are the bridge-makers. It is my hope that those who use this book will be inspired to support and honor their origins and be motivated to leave a rich legacy to the children of the Earth and the generations of the future.

Angeles Arrien
Sausalito, California
1992

DECLARATION*

We the Indigenous Peoples of the world, united in this corner of our Mother the Earth in a great assembly of men of wisdom, declare to all nations:

We glory in our proud past:

> when the earth was our nurturing mother,
>
> when the night sky formed our common roof,
>
> when Sun and Moon were our parents,
>
> when all were brothers and sisters,
>
> when our great civilizations grew under the sun,
>
> when our chiefs and elders were great leaders,
>
> when justice ruled the Law and its execution.

Then other peoples arrived:

> thirsting for blood, for gold, for land and all its wealth,
>
> carrying the cross and the sword, one in each hand,
>
> without knowing or waiting to learn the ways of our worlds,
>
> they considered us to be lower than the animals,
>
> they stole our land from us and took us from our lands,
>
> they made slaves of the Sons of the sun.

* Source: Douglas E. Sanders, *The Formation of the World Council of Indigenous Peoples,* IWGIA Document No. 29, 1977. This declaration was agreed upon by the delegates to the first international conference of Indigenous Peoples in Port Alberni, British Columbia, in 1975, which led to the establishment of the World Council of Indigenous Peoples (WCIP).

However, they have never been able to eliminate us,
    nor to erase our memories of what we were,
    because we are the culture of the earth and the sky,
    we are of ancient descent and we are millions,
    and although our whole universe may be ravaged,
    our people will live on
    for longer than even the kingdom of death.

Now, we come from the four corners of the earth,
    we protest before the concert of nations
    that, "we are the Indigenous Peoples, we who
    have a consciousness of culture and peoplehood
    on the edge of each country's borders and
    marginal to each country's citizenship."

And rising up after centuries of oppression,
    evoking the greatness of our ancestors,
    in the memory of our Indigenous martyrs,
    and in homage to the counsel of our wise elders:

We vow to control again our own destiny and
    recover our complete humanity and
    pride in being Indigenous People.

INTRODUCTION

*Indigenous peoples are one of the world's most
persistent voices of conscience, alerting humankind
to the dangers of environmental destruction.
And as the world searches for alternative strategies
to deal with global problems, it is turning more
and more to indigenous peoples. Much of their respect
for nature, their methods of resource management,
social organization, values, and culture are finding
echoes in the writings of scientists, philosophers,
politicians, and thinkers.*

—Julian Burger, *The Gaia Atlas of First Peoples:
A Future for the Indigenous World*

Today it is imperative that we pay attention to ecological issues. Our planet, the house we live in, is in danger of becoming unlivable, due primarily to the neglect of our own industrialized society. It is clear that we need to take action for change before it is too late.

Our word *ecology* comes from the Greek word *oikos*, which means "house." As we move into the twenty-first century, it is the work of all human beings to attend to the health of both our "inner" and "outer" houses: the inner house of our selves, the limitless world within, and the outer house of the world in which we live our daily lives. Many people in contemporary society feel little or no connection between these two worlds, a state that the indigenous, land-based peoples of the earth, whose cultures reach back thousands of years, would find not only sad but incomprehensible. In *Voices of the First Day*, Robert Lawlor quotes an aboriginal tribal elder saying, "They say we have been here for 60,000 years, but it is much longer. We have been here since the time before time began. We have come directly out of the Dreamtime of the Creative Ancestors. We have lived and kept the earth as it was on the First Day." And it is to native peoples that we can now look for guidance on how to care for the earth as if it were its first day. Their universal, ancient wisdoms can help restore balance within our own nature, and assist in rebalancing the needs of the natural environment.

We live in an age that is calling for a "new world order." Our current world order actually consists of four worlds: (1) the highly industrialized First World countries, such as the United States and the nations of Western Europe; (2) the Second World socialist block nations; (3) the developing countries of the Third World, such as Brazil or Thailand; and (4) the Fourth World, which George Manuel of the World Council of Indigenous Peoples describes in the *Gaia Atlas of First Peoples* (Burger) as the "name given to indigenous peoples descended from a country's aboriginal population and who today are completely or partly deprived of the right to their own territory and riches. The peoples of the Fourth World have only limited influence or none at all in the national state to which they belong." The differences between these worlds can be stated very simply: The First, Second, and Third Worlds believe that "the land belongs to the people"; the Fourth World believes that "the people belong to the land." A new world order can be created once all four worlds create a bridge that is truly healing. Perhaps this bridge can be the interface where these four worlds meet in joining together to heal and restore Mother Earth.

For the people of the first three worlds, understanding and accepting the belief of the Fourth World is the first and most crucial step in creating a truly new and healing "new world order." This may seem impossible, but it is not. The interface between the worlds is not rigid and impenetrable. As noted psychologist William Bridges explains,

Interface means "where the surface of one thing meets the surface of another. It is less like a dividing line and more like a permeable membrane, and the action at the interface is the interplay, the communication, the mutual influence that goes on between societies . . . that are side by side. The interface is where the vital relationships are established that are necessary for survival in a world of increasing interdependency."

Becoming Change Masters

For many people the ideals of the Industrial Revolution— toward more progress, more development, and greater wealth —no longer seem relevant, yet we have trouble letting them go. But if we are to survive in the twenty-first century, we must reconsider our priorities.

In *Dreaming the Dark*, Starhawk reminds us, "Directed energy causes change. To have integrity, we must recognize that our choices bring consequences, and that we cannot escape responsibility for the consequences, not because they are imposed by some external authority, but because they are inherent in the choices themselves." Indigenous and Eastern cultures have long recognized that the only constant is change, and that the principle of interdependence is essential for survival. Among tribal peoples medicine men and women, chiefs, shamans, teachers, and seers are the "change masters," a term Rosabeth Moss Kanter introduced in her 1985 book *The Change Masters*. The shamanic traditions, practiced by agrarian and indigenous peoples the world over, remind us that for centuries human beings have used the wisdom of nature and ritual to support change and life transitions rather than to ignore or deny life processes, as we so often do.

Our society, like many other Western societies, is alienated from its mythological roots. In the Introduction to Arnold Van Gennep's *Rites of Passage*, Salon Kimbala suggests that "one dimension of mental illness may arise because an increasing number of individuals are forced to accomplish their traditions alone with private symbols." This alienation process may be alleviated by relearning the ways of our ancestors. David Feinstein, in an article in the *American Journal of Orthopsychiatry*, reminds us that renewal requires a return to the basic source from which all personal and cultural myths are ultimately forged: the human psyche.

No matter what world we live in now, we are all people of the earth, connected to one another by our mutual humanity. When we listen to land-based peoples, we are listening to our oldest selves. Indigenous cultures support change and healing, transition and rites of passage, through mythic structures and through the incorporation into daily life of art, science, music, ritual, and drama. Every culture in the world has singing, dancing, and storytelling, and these are practices to which we all have access. We also have access to the four inner archetypes, or blueprints for human behavior, which are present in the mythic structure of societies the world over.

LIVING THE FOUR-FOLD WAY

Grandfather, Great Spirit, . . . You have set the powers of the four quarters of the earth to cross each other. You have made me cross the good road, and the road of difficulties, and where they cross, the place is holy. Day in, day out, forevermore, you are the life of things.
—Black Elk, Oglala Sioux (Nerburn, *Native American Wisdom*)

My research has demonstrated that virtually all shamanic traditions draw on the power of four archetypes in order to live in harmony and balance with our environment and with our own inner nature: the Warrior, the Healer, the Visionary, and the Teacher. Because each archetype draws on the deepest mythic roots of humanity, we too can tap into their wisdom. When we learn to live these archetypes within ourselves, we will begin to heal ourselves and our fragmented world.

The following four principles, each based on an archetype, comprise what I call the Four-Fold Way:

1. *Show up, or choose to be present.* Being present allows us to access the human resources of power, presence, and communication. This is the way of the Warrior.

2. *Pay attention to what has heart and meaning.* Paying attention opens us to the human resources of love, gratitude, acknowledgment, and validation. This is the way of the Healer.

3. *Tell the truth without blame or judgment.* Nonjudgmental truthfulness maintains our authenticity, and develops our inner vision and intuition. This is the way of the Visionary.

4. *Be open to outcome, not attached to outcome.* Openness and nonattachment help us recover the human resources of wisdom and objectivity. This is the way of the Teacher.

When we understand these universal experiences, we are better able to respect the diverse ways in which these shared themes are expressed by all people. Even though these four archetypes are emphasized in most shamanic traditions, it is important to understand that they are universal and available to all humankind, regardless of context, culture, structure, and practice. In our society we express the way of the Warrior in our leadership ability. We express the way of the Healer through our attitudes toward maintaining our own health and the health of our environment. We express the way of the Visionary through our personal creativity, and through our ability to bring our life dreams and visions into the world. We express the way of the Teacher through our constructive communication and informational skills.

How to Use This Book

In many shamanic traditions, optimum health is considered to be the equal expression of these archetypes. Indigenous peoples consider it vitally important to be balanced in all four areas: leading, healing, visioning, and teaching. For most people, however, this balance is far from a reality. Most of us tend to over-express one area, while leaving the others undeveloped. Take a moment to assess your own balance. Do you consider yourself a Warrior, a Healer, a Visionary, or a Teacher?

If you think of yourself as a Warrior or leader, for example, do you feel fully competent in this area, or would learning the skills of the Visionary help you express your vision of what might be possible? Would learning the skills of the Healer help you work with people out of love rather than out of competition? Would learning the skills of the Teacher open you to new directions you have not considered? In this book we'll explore ways to open to the full power of each way.

This book is divided into four parts. Within each part we will explore the theory and practice of each archetype. Theory includes the guiding principle of the archetype, tools you can use for empowerment, how you can use nature to connect with the archetype, and how you might be expressing the negative aspects of the archetype, or what psychologist Carl Jung called the *shadow*.

The practice section includes a posture to help you understand and express the archetype through your body as well as your mind, and questions to help you explore further on your own. These questions, as the word itself suggests, are designed to take you on a quest for the archetype that lies dormant within you. Do not be afraid to venture into areas that are unknown, unclear, unexplored, unexpressed. Use the questions in any way you wish. If you keep a journal, you may want to write the answers there. If you meditate, you may decide to meditate on them. Please ask and answer the questions many times; your answers will begin to change as the archetypes begin to develop and find expression within you. Finally, each section ends with a summary, and a chart that shows the natural associations of each archetype.

Cave art and ancient designs were selected as the art motif throughout the book, because every continent has cave art. These designs, which seem at once ancient and modern, serve to remind us all of humanity's deeper origins.

My research and the research of many others has shown me that the thought of indigenous peoples everywhere is remarkably consistent. This book is intended not as a scholarly reference, but as an entryway into Fourth World consciousness for people of the first three worlds. For this reason I refer throughout this book to cross-cultural ideas and truths. If you would like to read more about the specific practices of individual cultures, please refer to the Bibliography for more information.

Embarking on the Four-Fold Way

Spiritualism is the highest form of political consciousness. The native peoples of the West are among the world's surviving proprietors of that kind of consciousness. They are here to impart that message. It is important to use it wisely and well as we go into the twenty-first century—a time of bridging ancient wisdoms into the creative tapestry of contemporary times.

THE WAY OF THE WARRIOR

People are like tea bags.
You find out how strong they are
when you put them in hot water.

—Anonymous

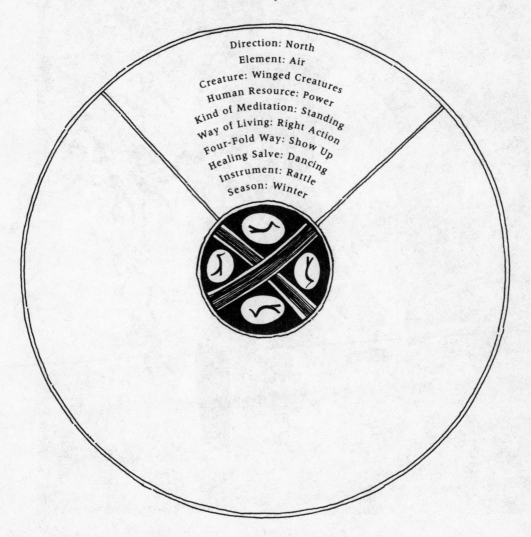

Direction: North
Element: Air
Creature: Winged Creatures
Human Resource: Power
Kind of Meditation: Standing
Way of Living: Right Action
Four-Fold Way: Show Up
Healing Salve: Dancing
Instrument: Rattle
Season: Winter

Cross-culturally, there are many different perspectives from the indigenous peoples of each continent regarding the directions and seasons. However, the majority view them as presented here.

SHOWING UP AND CHOOSING TO BE PRESENT

Indigenous societies throughout the world connect to the process of empowerment through the mythic theme and archetypal expression of the Warrior. Throughout history men and women who have explored the way of the Warrior have been called leaders, protectors, sorcerers, adventurers, and explorers. In contemporary Western society, becoming an effective leader in any field of endeavor means developing the inner Warrior.

The principle that guides the Warrior is *showing up and choosing to be present*. The developed Warrior shows *honor and respect* for all things, employs *judicious communication, sets limits and boundaries,* is *responsible and disciplined,* demonstrates *right use of power,* and understands *the three universal powers.*

Honor and Respect

Perhaps the most important aspect of the Warrior is the ability to extend honor and respect. *Honor* is the capacity to confer respect to another individual. We become honorable when our capacities for respect are expressed and strengthened. The term *respect* comes from the Latin word *respicere,* which means "the willingness to look again." The Warrior is willing to take a second look rather than remain stuck in a particular view of a situation or individual.

If we want to access the Warrior archetype and become more effective leaders, we must be willing to look at our many real abilities rather than fixate on just one or two parts of who we think we are. Successful leaders are able to appreciate the diversity within themselves and others. The coach of a championship team, for example, gets the best from players by placing them at different positions to assess their potential rather than insisting they always play the position for which they were hired.

When we are willing to look again, we extend respect. This allows us to stay open and flexible toward ourselves and others.

Judicious Communication

The skillful Warrior who knows how to extend honor and respect begins to value the art and craft of *communication*. The effective leader is consistent in words and action.

There are two causes for all misunderstandings: not saying what we mean, and not doing what we say. When we say what we mean and do what we say, we become trustworthy. Many indigenous societies recognize that a lack of alignment between word and action always results in a loss of power and effectiveness. Chief Sitting Bull, quoted in volume 1 of Roger Moody's *The Indigenous Voice*, describes what happens when respect is not extended and when words and actions are not consistent:

. . . outwardly, he stands in physical readiness for any call to service, and inwardly, he strives to fulfill the Way. . . . Within his heart he keeps to the ways of peace, but without he keeps his weapons ready for use.
—Ryusaku Tsunoda,
Sources of Japanese Tradition

What treaty that the whites have kept has the red man broken? Not one.

What treaty that the white man ever made with us have they kept? Not one.

When I was a boy the Sioux owned the world; the sun rose and set on their land; they sent ten thousand men to battle. Where are the warriors today? Who slew them? Where are our lands? Who owns them? What white man can say I ever stole his land or a penny of his money? Yet, they say I am a thief. What white woman, however lonely, was ever captive or insulted by me? Yet they say I am a bad Indian. What white man has ever seen me drunk? Who has ever come to me hungry and unfed? Who has ever seen me beat my wives or abuse my children? What law have I broken? Is it wrong for me to love my own? Is it wicked for me because my skin is red? Because I am a Sioux; because I was born where my father lived; because I would die for my people and my country?

Regardless of our cultural identity, it is important to consider the personal and professional treaties we have kept and honored, and those we have broken. Children recognize the importance of keeping trust by honoring contracts when they cry, "But you broke your promise!"

Limits and Boundaries

Another aspect of communication that is necessary for effective leadership is the ability to understand the difference between *yes* and *no*. These two words reveal our limits and boundaries—what we are willing to do and what we are not willing to do. When we say "yes" when we mean "no," we lose personal power and become victims or martyrs. When we say "no" to someone else when we know the situation calls for us to say "yes," we become stingy or selfish.

Unfortunately, the Western mind often believes that the word "yes" means "I like you and agree with you," and the word "no" means "I'm rejecting you or disagreeing with you." Most people in the non-Western world, however, don't overlay these words with emotional intent. They recognize that "yes" acknowledges a viewpoint or perspective and does not necessarily mean agreement; and that "no" simply honors a limit and a boundary and indicates the ability to respect what one is willing to do or not do at this point in time.

Never spend time with people who don't respect you.
—Maori proverb
(Feldman, *A World Treasury*)

The Warrior's way demands that we honor and respect our personal limits and boundaries as well as the limits and boundaries of others. The effective leader knows how to be a flexible negotiator by being able to say appropriately, "No, this is a limit," and "Yes, this is something I'm willing to do."

Responsibility and Discipline

The Warrior must also understand and be aware of the causes and effects of actions taken or not taken. This capacity of attention is called *responsibility,* "the ability to respond." The Chinese *Book of Changes,* the *I Ching,* reminds us that "it is not the event that is important, it is the response to the event that is everything." Responsibility is not only the ability to respond to what comes toward us, it is also the capacity to stand behind our actions and to be responsible for all that we do or don't do. This means that we do not allow ourselves to be in denial about ourselves, or to be self-indulgent. Our ability to respond impeccably and with integrity to the events we create brings us into the Warrior's arena.

This aspect of responsibility is *discipline.* Discipline is the process of facing life directly and acting without haste. The word "discipline" actually means "being a disciple unto oneself." When we are disciples unto ourselves, we honor our own rhythm, our step-by-step nature. We are most likely to be thrown off course when we have too much to do or too little to do. These times should act as reminders to engage discipline, to move not rashly but step by step.

Discipline and responsibility are the Warrior's tools for honoring structure and function. Land-based peoples know that too much structure or form leads to rigidity and calcification, and that too much function or random creativity leads to chaos. In the Orient the balance between structure and function is expressed by the metaphor of the bamboo reed—the capacity to be firm yet yielding. Ancient societies recognize the inherent structure and function found in nature, and are committed to maintaining and recapturing nature's balance. The Warrior's way is to respect and protect the structure and function of Mother Nature. When we become stewards of the earth, we tap the archetype of the Warrior and take responsibility for how we use our power.

Thomas Cleary's *Zen Lessons: The Art of Leadership* is a collection of political, social, and psychological teachings of Chinese Zen (Chan) adepts of the Song Dynasty. In it we are reminded that if we adhere to the "three don'ts of leadership" we will not only be responsible, but we will also honor the processes of discipline found in all structures and functions:

> In Leadership there are three don'ts:
>
> > when there is much to do, don't be afraid;
> >
> > when there is nothing to do, don't be hasty; and
> >
> > don't talk about opinions of right and wrong.
>
> A leader who succeeds in these things won't be confused or deluded by external objects.

When we apply the guidelines of the "three don'ts" in our lives, we honor the inherent aspects of structure and function by instilling discipline and responsibility into all that we do.

Right Use of Power

The challenge of every Warrior and leader is *the right use of power.* Native peoples of the American continents use the words *power* and *medicine* synonymously. If we fully express who we are, we are said to be "full of power" and "expressing our medicine."

Power is a human resource that is often equated with the use of energy or the empowerment of self and others. When we demonstrate our power, no one can tell us what can't be done. We are freed from patterns of self-diminishment and are less likely to accept other people's perceptions of what we can and cannot do. In mythological terms the problematic suggestions that we give ourselves and others are known as *spells*, magical incantations that govern our behavior. Common spells include the words, "I can't," "I wish I would have," "Someday I'll," and "If only." Lewis Carroll's famous masterpiece *Through the Looking Glass* (quoted from Van Ekeren, *The Speaker's Sourcebook*) contains a conversation between Alice and the queen. The queen, in a warrior-like way, acknowledges personal power and does not allow self-imposed spells or the suggestions of others to interfere with what is to be done. She reinforces the need to dream the impossible dream:

> "I can't believe that!" said Alice.
>
> "Can't you?" the queen said in a pitying tone. "Try again, draw a long breath, and shut your eyes."
>
> Alice laughed. "There's no use trying," she said. "One can't believe impossible things."
>
> "I daresay you haven't had much practice," said the queen. "When I was your age, I always did it for half an hour a day. Why, sometimes I've believed as many as six impossible things before breakfast."

Many indigenous societies believe that we all possess "original medicine": personal power, duplicated nowhere else on the planet. No two individuals carry the same combination of talents or challenges; therefore, when we compare ourselves to others, native peoples see this as a sign that we do not believe that we have original medicine. This belief affects not only ourselves, but extends into the world. Not to be "in our medicine" or bring our power into the world precludes healing from coming to Mother Nature and all her creatures.

Eastern societies honor right use of power through martial arts and working with their own *ki* or *ch'i*, the power that is derived from the life force. In Cleary's *Zen Lessons*, every leader is reminded about the ingredients that are necessary in the right use of power: "The body of leadership has four limbs: enlightenment and virtue, speech and action, humaneness and justice, etiquette and law." The archetype of the Warrior requires us to use power in an enlightened way that incorporates integrity, alignment of speech and action, honor and respect, and serves humanity fairly and justly. The leader who expects people to perform to the best of their ability will achieve the greatest result. The right use of power allows us to empower ourselves and others.

Three Universal Powers

My research has shown that universally there are three kinds of power: power of presence, power of communication, and power of position. People in shamanic societies believe that a person who has all three powers embodies "big medicine" and cannot be ignored.

Three famous individuals who carry these powers, and who draw on the mythical structure and archetype of the way of the Warrior/Leader, are Eleanor Roosevelt, Gandhi, and Martin Luther King, Jr. Each is an example of how a person can embody the power of presence, the power of communication, and the power of position by being willing to take a stand in an arena that has heart and meaning for them. In shamanic societies it is the Warrior's task to become visible, and through example and intention to empower and inspire others. It is important to remember that people who carry big medicine can be found in all walks of life, and may not necessarily be well known.

Power of Presence

Every human being carries the power of presence. Walt Whitman recognized this power when he wrote in *Leaves of Grass*, "We convince by our presence." Many indigenous societies recognize this capacity, often referred to as "showing up" or "choosing to be present and visible."

The power of presence means we are able to bring all four intelligences forward: mental, emotional, spiritual, and physical. Some individuals carry such presence that we identify them as charismatic or magnetic personalities. We are drawn to them; they captivate our interest even before they speak or we know anything about them.

It's easy to choose not to be present: We may drift off in our thoughts, be emotionally embroiled in a past problem, or be dreaming about future possibilities. In this case it can be truly said that we're "not all there." When we choose to "show up" energetically, with all four intelligences, we express the power of presence.

Fame or integrity: which is more important?

Money or happiness: which is more valuable?

Success or failure: which is more destructive?

Mastering others is strength;

Mastering yourself is true power.

When you are content to be simply yourself and don't compare or compete, everyone will respect you.

—Lao Tzu, Tao Te Ching (Mitchell)

Power of Communication

Effective communication is the Warrior's or leader's way. Skillful communication means we have aligned content, timing, and context. Blunt communication is an announcement of great content, but poor timing and context. Confused communication often carries good timing and context but poor content, and leads to incongruity between our words and our behavior.

For communication to carry maximum effectiveness, we need to be consistent in the essential communication ingredients: word choice, tonality, and nonverbal body language. For example, we may make an excellent word choice, such as, "This is a terrific day"; but our dreary tone and hanging head may send the contradictory message that it is not such a terrific day. Communication that empowers and inspires us is communication that is delivered at the appropriate time and place for the person involved to hear and receive it.

"Then you should say what you mean," the March Hare went on. "I do," Alice hastily replied; "at least . . . I mean what I say—that's the same thing, you know."

—Lewis Carroll, *Alice's Adventures in Wonderland*

Power of Position

The Warrior demonstrates the willingness to take a stand. This is the capacity to let others know where we stand, where we don't stand, what we stand for, and how we stand up for ourselves.

Many politicians have great presence and great communication, but lose power when they leave people wondering where they stand on specific issues. Hindu yogic postures, shamanic "power spots," and *feng shui* (the Chinese concept of correct placement of buildings and their furnishings) all recognize the power of position. Many native cultures use these four principles as a guideline for leading a life of quality and integrity. A true Warrior/Leader is identified as someone who knows how to extend honor and respect; set limits and boundaries; align words with actions; and extend responsibility into structure and function in an empowering way.

EMPOWERMENT TOOLS OF THE WARRIOR

Shamanic cultures have a variety of apprenticeship and training for developing these leadership and empowerment skills. For many indigenous cultures, *soul retrieval work* is an empowerment skill employed by those who desire to bring lost parts of themselves back home. Sandra Ingerman in her book *Soul Retrieval* describes this ancient methodology. The empowerment tools used in this work include *rattle work, dancing, standing meditation,* and *power animals and helping allies.*

Rattle Work

The use of sonics, inducing sound with instruments, to create an altered state is an important part of soul retrieval work in shamanic traditions. The oldest musical instrument used for soul retrieval work among native peoples is the *rattle*, humankind's imitation of rain. It is a cleansing and purification instrument used to remedy "soul loss." Contemporary terms for soul loss include "depression," "disheartenment," and "dispiritedness." In practice, most shamans first use the rattle for cleansing and purifying. Then they use the rattle's sound to call parts of the soul that have been lost in the past, in a particular place, or in an old relationship.

Most shamanic societies attribute three functions to the rattle: (1) soul retrieval work, (2) cleansing and purifying, and (3) assisting visionary work (this is done by asking the rattle, through its sound, for any oracular guidance that may be needed). Even today the rattle remains the one object that family and friends universally give to all newborn infants. Perhaps human beings carry a subliminal recognition of the rattle as a primal source of comfort, revitalization, and power that is still present in contemporary times to remind us to reclaim and remember all the parts of who we are.

Dancing

Dancing is a method for empowerment and soul retrieval work that is used consciously or subconsciously by all societies. When we dance we touch the essence of who we are and experience the unity between spirit and matter. As Alonzo Quavehema of the Hopi people explains (as quoted in James K. Page, Jr.'s *Rare Glimpse into the Evolving Way of the Hopi*), "We stay up and sing the sacred songs all night to purify ourselves so that our dancing and our prayers can do good for everyone."

Today we can use dance therapy to get in touch with the Warrior within. A good example of this type of Warrior work is described by professional dancer Gabrielle Roth in her book *Maps to Ecstasy*, in which she teaches the five rhythms that are elemental when any human being explores dance:

1. The *flowing rhythm* is a teacher of fluidity and grace.

2. The *rhythm of chaos* is an announcement of creativity seeking a form.

3. The *staccato rhythm* is the teacher of definition and refinement.

4. The *lyrical rhythm* is the teacher of synthesis and integration.

5. The *rhythm of stillness* is the teacher of contentment and peace.

When we are comfortable with all five rhythms, the separation between inner and outer experience is closed. Folk wisdom from East Africa describes the essence of this unity by saying, "One leg cannot dance alone" (Feldman, *A World Treasury of Folk Wisdom*).

Standing Meditation

The Warrior uses the rhythm of stillness to integrate the powers of presence, communication, and position. Shamanic

With time even a bear can learn to dance.
—Yiddish proverb
(Feldman, *A World Treasury*)

traditions use the standing posture and the rhythm of stillness to train people in the art of coming into the full power of themselves. It is not uncommon in these societies for individuals to pray for long periods of time in a standing posture during vision quests. Cross-culturally, the posture of *standing meditation* (described in Processes and Reminders, p. 37) is used in martial arts, spiritual practices, and the military as a way of reinforcing and coalescing the three universal powers of presence, communication, and position, which allows us to connect with the greater being of who we are. In his classic guide to leadership, influence, and excellence, *Tao Te Ching* (quoted from R. L. Wing's translation, *The Tao of Power*), Lao Tzu reminds us of the Warrior's way of using and understanding power and the dance of life:

> To know the absolute is to be tolerant.
> What is tolerant becomes impartial;
> What is impartial becomes powerful;
> What is powerful becomes natural;
> What is natural becomes Tao.

The search for the full-functioning self promises to be the most fruitful endeavor a leader can undertake. To be full of power—powerful—is the natural, tolerant, respectful, and impartial stance of the Warrior's way.

Power Animals and Helping Allies

Many shamanic societies access power by consciously working with a *power animal*. Our power animal is that animal with which we most identify, or which has made itself known to us in our dreams, meditative practices, or shamanic journey work at least four times. Its function is to guard and protect our physical body. It calls in the *helping allies* (the animals that we are consistently drawn to in our lives or with which we feel resonance) to assist during times of transition, growth, and deepening.

The power animal and helping allies assist us daily in the tests or challenges that we face. In those cultures that have totems, they may be symbolized as carved power animals that protect the village or community; carved histories of the family and community with their guardian spirits, as is the case among Pacific Northwest native peoples; or empowerment objects, with an image of the individual's power animal at the base and images of any additional animals layered on top as the helping allies. In his innovative and empowering book *The Personal Totem Pole*, Stephen Gallegos demonstrates how to combine totems, animal imagery, and *chakras*, or energy center work, in the psychotherapeutic context, using animal imagery as a way to connect with one's own healing nature.

THE WARRIOR'S CONNECTION TO NATURE

Native peoples recognize that the most empowering and healing tool that we have available to us is our *connection to nature and the wilderness.* In his book *Indian Country*, Peter Matthiessen reminds us of the deep connection between nature and spirit:

> Man is an aspect of nature, and nature itself is a manifestation of primordial religion. Even the word "religion" makes an unnecessary separation, and there is no word for it in the Indian tongues. Nature is the "Great Mysterious," the "religion before religion"...

Built into the vision quests, or ceremonialized wilderness experiences of native peoples, is the inherent knowledge that nature is an unlimited resource for empowerment and for connecting spirit with matter. Biologically, in order to maintain our vitality and energy levels, it is imperative to be outdoors for one full hour every day. As children we spent more time outdoors than we did indoors; and as adults we spend more time indoors than outdoors. To maintain our well-being, it is necessary to our vitality and spirit to connect daily with natural light, air, and earth. In their cave art, Neolithic societies represented the biological need

for human beings to be connected to nature by the repeated drawings of individuals as trees, or what appear to be "tree people."

Among many indigenous cultures, *trees* are regarded as the medicine people of the plant kingdom. Like trees, the Warrior's way is to become rooted and contained—flexible and bending in the wind, yet stable. In many cultures trees symbolize the process of transformation. The roots of the trees are associated with the past and how we honor our heritage and ancestors. The trunk symbolizes the present life and reveals where the life force and creative spirit are either engaged or not. The branches symbolize desired future goals, or if it is a flowering or fruit tree, the attainment of those goals. The Warrior, like a tree, honors the past, present, and future from season to season.

Another Warrior empowerment tool that is used for stabilizing and containing energy is the *standing posture combined with hand positions.* These hand positions involve placing one hand over the heart, and placing the other hand between the ribcage and the navel. In the valleys of Uzbekistan, this posture asks for the help of a group of spirits called Chiltan, who are called upon to heal, to restore power, and to stabilize energy. Felicitas D. Goodman has studied the cross-cultural postures that induce trance journeys and ecstatic experiences. In her book *Where the Spirits Ride the Wind*, she explains that the Chiltan posture has turned up on the Northwest coast of North America, in Arizona, in ancient Europe, in modern Africa, and among the Olmecs in Central America. In Hindu societies working with both hand positions

Spontaneous me, Nature,
The loving day,
the mounting sun,
the friend I am happy
    with . . .
—Walt Whitman, "Song of
Myself," *Complete Poetry*

(*mudras*) and varied body postures (*yoga*) is the method that is most used for rebalancing energy or personal power. These postures are found in many cultures, both ancient and contemporary. Recognition of these simple empowerment tools and their continuing practice are important for the development of the inner Warrior.

Other nature metaphors and symbols that are attributed to the way of the Warrior are the *sky*, the *four winds*, the *sun*, the *moon*, and the *stars*. Many native peoples attribute the way of the Warrior to the direction of the *North*, the home of *Father Sky*, and all *birds* and winged creatures. *Winter* is the season that is most attributed among some shamanic societies to the direction of the North. Winter is the season for incubation, gestation, and consolidation.

Although Winter does not universally entail ice and snow, each hemisphere has its own Winter season of rest. During this season many indigenous societies complete that which is unfinished. Winter is the season for reflection and contemplation. It is considered to be the best time to prepare for the renewal and healing that are provided in the season of Spring. When we are tested, it is important to embrace our challenges with the dignity, power, and grace of the "winged ones."

Ancient empowerment tools, such as practicing the Chiltan posture or standing like tree people, help us become present and be fully visible. Modern-day stress-reduction and relaxation techniques also provide ways for us, as Western urban dwellers, to center ourselves. Planting trees, gardening, or having small container gardens are ways that we re-green our own natures by connecting to the plant kingdom.

How the Unclaimed Warrior/Leader Reveals Itself: The Shadow Aspects of the Warrior Archetype, The Wounded Child of the North

When we are not fully present or empowered, we find ourselves caught in the shadow of the Warrior archetype. We have not claimed the Warrior or leader within our nature if we see in our lives the themes of rebellion, unclaimed authority or projecting our authority onto others, and patterns of invisibility.

Rebellion

Rebels are not just revolutionaries; they can be you, or me, or your next-door neighbor—anyone who has within them the overwhelming need to make a mark by doing things differently from the norm. Rebels cannot tolerate being ordinary. They are often incapable of working within established structures and forms. Rebels honor their own personal and professional needs above anyone else's, regardless of whether it is the appropriate time, place, or situation to do so. For rebels to become Warriors, they need to learn how to honor and respect the limits and boundaries of others, to take responsibility for actions taken or not taken, and to claim leadership in a way that empowers people rather than diminishes them.

The rebel is over-identified with being independent and self-sufficient. Behind every rebel is a need for space. The underlying fear for the rebel is the fear of being limited, restricted, or restrained. The rebel who uses leadership skills for personal gains faces diminished skill in being a team player, and eventually loses the respect of others. Taken to the extreme, the rebel becomes the narcissist and abandons effective leadership.

Authority Issues

When we have an *authority issue* with someone, we have not fully owned the Warrior archetype and we are projecting our authority onto someone else rather than claiming it. People with authority issues are drawn to effective leaders and have a tendency either to over-idealize them or to compete with them. Behind every individual who has an authority issue is the unwillingness to claim personal responsibility, and often an unconscious desire to have someone else be responsible.

Any authority issue reveals an individual who is behaving like a victim. For example, when an authority figure does not meet an individual's idealized expectations, a victim

THE FOUR-FOLD WAY

will counter with blame, judgment, and attack; or will respond with disappointment, avoidance, and withdrawal. The victim who uses blame is beginning to reclaim personal authority in a convoluted way, using leadership skills to attack or self-justify. The victim who uses withdrawal or avoidance is unsuccessfully attempting to reclaim personal authority.

A person who claims personal authority is no longer a victim. As we claim our own authority, these convoluted ways of owning power are disengaged. We begin to value collaboration with colleagues and honor people who demonstrate effective leadership skills.

Patterns of Invisibility

We often avoid reclaiming personal power by participating in *patterns of invisibility.* These patterns include hiding or holding back or "riding on the coattails" of powerful people. Low self-esteem and the inability to see oneself correctly is often at the root of the pattern of hiding or holding back. Another form of remaining invisible is to influence situations from behind the scenes.

If we carry this particular pattern of hiding, we fear exposure or being fully seen in areas where we are inherently talented. Hiding behind the scenes reveals difficulty demonstrating personal leadership qualities and creative expression. This is very different than being fully behind someone else's creative efforts with our own gifts and talents fully engaged and not compromised in any way. "Riding on the coattails" of powerful people reveals an individual's tendency to claim power vicariously rather than using personal leadership skills directly. Being in the light of someone else's power gives us the illusion that we are in our own power when we are not. Underneath all patterns of invisibility is the fear of exposure and accountability. These fears spring from self-worth issues and affect the individual's ability to fully engage in life.

If these shadow aspects are highly developed in any category, leadership skills of equal magnitude are waiting to be claimed. Courage and bravery are the keys for exploring and embracing all aspects of the Warrior archetype; by accessing the quality of courage, we can claim full leadership. The ultimate demonstration of courage is the call for peace. Ten Bears, a Yamparika Comanche (quoted in Nerburn and Mengelkoch's *Native American Wisdom*), models the Warrior archetype with his prayer: "Great Spirit—I want no blood upon my land to stain the grass, I want it all clear and pure, and I wish it so, that all who go through among my people may find it peaceful when they come, and leave peacefully when they go."

It is the Warrior's way to embrace strengths and weaknesses. With all parts of ourselves embraced, illusions are more easily collapsed. This enables us to participate in life more fully. As Joan of Arc, the fifteenth-century mystic, said, "In God's name! Let us go on bravely!"

PROCESSES AND REMINDERS: IMPORTANT PRACTICES TO DEVELOP THE INNER WARRIOR

1. *Spend at least fifteen minutes each day in standing meditation.* Record your experience in your journal or create a special meditation log.

Standing Meditation

Accessing the Inner Warrior

Accessing the Quality of Presence and Inner Authority

Purpose

The purpose of standing meditation is to honor sacred time. This is a time set aside for introspection, contemplation, discovery, and honoring the sacred or divine.

Posture

Stand with your head erect, your arms at your sides, and your feet placed shoulder-width apart. Your eyes should be open, and fixed softly on a distant point.

This meditation posture is found in Oriental, Asian, Tibetan, and shamanistic practices. In some Western practices, standing postures are incorporated with kneeling and sitting postures.

Process

Within this sacred time and posture, you can feel what it is like to stand up for yourself: literally to have two feet on the ground, to take a stand, to stand on your own two feet. In standing meditation you experience what it means to set limits and to come from a place of self-respect and self-esteem.

Standing meditation is an opportunity to access your presence, personal power, and authority, and to experience the inner Warrior. In the East the Warrior is an individual who has the ability to honor and respect self and others (as demonstrated, for example, in the martial arts of Aikido and Tai Chi). Expressing the inner Warrior means being aware and present without effort or holding back. It is the capacity to own your presence and personal power without giving it away or deflecting it. In standing meditation you experience what it means to work from a posture of respect: the willingness to "look again," at self and others, from a position of strength and flexibility.

2. *Spend one hour in nature or out-of-doors every day for maintenance of health and well-being.*

3. *Spend time doing soul retrieval work with the rattle.* Move the rattle up and down in front of your body in long vertical and horizontal motions. The rattle is humankind's imitation of rain, so this movement provides a cleansing and purification of your own nature. Now move the rattle in wide circular motions to the right side of your body; this will call back

lost parts of your dynamic nature. Do the same on the left side of your body, to call back lost parts of your magnetic nature.

4. *Set aside time daily for some kind of exercise, bodywork, or movement.* Many indigenous cultures use the power of movement (such as ceremonial dance, Chiltan postures, yoga, Tai Chi, or other martial arts) to awaken the inner Warrior. Today we use aerobics, running, swimming, gymnastics, walking, and other kinds of exercise to help maintain access to our leadership skills.

5. *Spend time each day being aware of how you handle unexpected events or surprises.* Something unexpected happens every day, but we need not be knocked off balance. As we learn to accept and work with them, these occurrences can teach us how to stay centered and flexible at the same time—a practice necessary for any effective leader.

6. *Spend time honoring the guidances of your power animal and helping allies.*

The color of the skin makes no difference. What is good and just for one is good and just for the other, and the Great Spirit made all men brothers.
I have a red skin, but my grandfather was a white man. What does it matter? It is not the color of the skin that makes me good or bad.
—White Shield, Arikara Chief, from Native American Wisdom

Summary of the Warrior Archetype

The Warrior is the archetype of leadership. We come into our leadership skills by staying in our power, by showing up and choosing to be present, by extending honor and respect, and by being responsible and accountable.

Warrior Empowerment Tools

- Rattle Work
- Dancing
- Standing Meditation
- Power Animals and Helping Allies
- Connection to nature:
  Chiltan postures

Shadow Aspects of the Warrior

- Rebellion
- Authority Issues
- Patterns of Invisibility:
  hiding or holding back
  working behind the scenes
  riding coattails of powerful people

THREE
UNIVERSAL
POWERS:
PRESENCE
COMMUNICATION
POSITION

Warrior's Way—Leadership Skills

- To honor and respect
- To align words with actions
- To respect limits and boundaries
- To be responsible and disciplined
- To demonstrate right use of power
- Three Don'ts of Leadership

Nature Metaphors Attributed to the Direction of the North

- Father Sky
- The four Winds
- The Sun, Moon and Stars
- Birds, the Winged Creatures
- Tree People

Questions

Think about your responses to the following questions. To develop the inner Warrior, ask and answer questions 1 and 2 daily.

1. *Is the good, true, and beautiful within me as strong as the whispers of diminishment? (Or, in contemporary psychological terms, Is my self-worth as strong as my self-critic?)* If you can answer "yes" to this question, you are ready to bring your power or original medicine into any situation. If you cannot answer "yes" to this question, then you need to work with the Warrior empowerment tools described in this chapter.

2. *Where in my life did I stop dancing? Where in my life did I stop singing? Where in my life did I stop being enchanted with stories? Where in my life did I become uncomfortable with the sweet territory of silence?* Many indigenous peoples believe that wherever in our lives we stopped dancing, singing, being enchanted with stories, or began experiencing difficulty with silence is where we began to experience soul loss or loss of spirit. Dancing is the Warrior's way to retrieve those parts of the self that are lost or unremembered. Work with Roth's five rhythms as a soul retrieval tool for self-empowerment.

3. *Who are the leaders and people who have carried the "Warrior spirit," who have inspired me and have been sources of empowerment in history and in contemporary times?* The people who inspire you do so because they mirror aspects of your own inner Warrior, reminding you of your own inherent leadership skills. Make a list or a visual collage of these people to

reinforce the Warrior's gifts within that are waiting to be claimed.

4. *Who are the people who have acknowledged me for my leadership skills? Who are the people who have chosen me to be a fellow team player?* When you are acknowledged or chosen for your leadership skills, this is a recognition of your original medicine, your inner Warrior.

5. *What have been my greatest challenges? How have I handled these challenges?* Review the major challenges that you have faced. Where did you begin to face them with your full power rather than avoid them or constrict in fear? The Warrior archetype teaches us that when we meet a challenge with our full power, we engage our leadership skills and exercise our inherent gifts. When we meet challenges with fear, we experience the shadow aspects of the Warrior.

6. *Of the three universal powers (the power of presence, the power of communication, and the power of position), which are developed and which are undeveloped?* When in your life were you conscious of the power of presence? When in your life did you experience your effectiveness or ineffectiveness with the power of communication? When in your life have you been conscious of the power of position? What can you do to develop the powers that you consider undeveloped?

7. *What specific leadership skills do I have? How am I currently demonstrating these skills within my family, within my creativity, within my work life?*

8. *Where do I lose my power? What particular people or situations ignite my lack of courage?* Where and with whom am I unable to bring who I am fully forward?

9. *Where do I stand up for myself, stand on my own two feet, take a stand, and know what it is I cannot stand?* The contexts in which you are able to do these things allow you to experience your self-esteem and the power of who you are. Whenever you are fully visible and know where you stand, you experience what it means to be in your power. Work with the practice of standing meditation as a way to contact your true self and to experience the Warrior archetype.

10. *What parts of myself are currently at war with each other? What is the major conflict that I am currently experiencing in my life? Where do I create misunderstandings in my life? Do I say what I mean? Do I do what I say?* The two major sources of misunderstanding that lead to conflict are not saying what we mean and not doing what we say. Take some time in standing meditation to ask for guidance in how you can align your actions with your words.

11. *How do I respond when there is too much to do? How do I respond when there is nothing to do?* Competent leadership is committed to maintaining balance by managing personal energy, time, and resources. Prehistoric cave art reveals the importance that was attributed to staying relaxed and centered. The Chiltan postures and the tree people motif show how early people helped prevent overextension in busy times and provided comfort in slack times. Nature was held by ancient peoples as a source of replenishment and renewal. Modern-day stress-reduction techniques do much the same thing. Remember the three don'ts of leadership: "When there's too much to do, don't be afraid; when there is nothing to do, don't be hasty; and don't talk about opinions of right or wrong. A leader who succeeds in these things won't be confused or deluded by external objects."

12. *In what ways do I extend honor and respect to myself and others? Am I aware of my own limits and boundaries? Do I honor and respect the limits and boundaries of others?*

13. *In what areas of my life do I see myself as responsible and accountable? In what areas of my life am I disciplined?* When you are not responsible or accountable for your life, you become subject to the will of others. When you lack discipline or are unable to be a "disciple unto yourself," you will experience confusion and chaos.

14. *What is my connection to nature and to animals? Do I spend at least one full hour out doors every day?* Good health and well-being requires us to spend at least one full hour out doors every day. Make time in your life to do this. *What are my favorite animals?* Our favorite animals, among some native traditions, are known as our helping allies. Can you identify your helping allies? *Is there a particular animal that I have liked or been drawn to since childhood?* Some indigenous peoples call this a "power animal." Do you have a power animal?

15. *Of the three shadow aspects of the Warrior, what patterns of invisibility have I explored? In what parts of my life have I been a rebel? In what parts of my life have I had authority issues? In what parts of my life have I experienced being a victim?* The shadow aspects of the Warrior archetype reveal aspects of leadership skills that are waiting to be claimed. Work with the Warrior empowerment tools described in this chapter to claim or liberate your trapped power.

THE WAY OF THE HEALER

Whatever house I enter,
I shall come to heal.

—The Hippocratic Oath

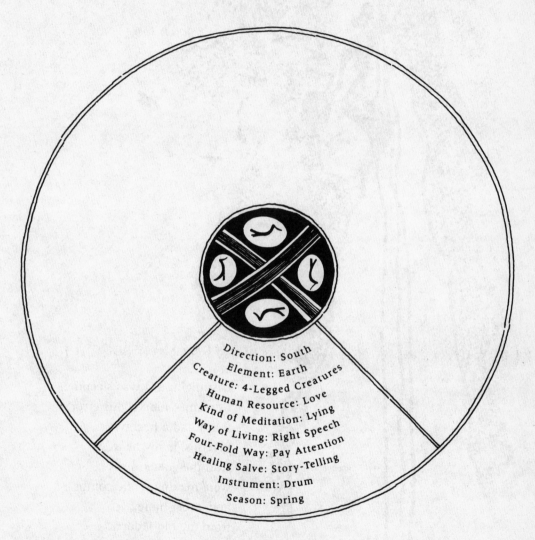

Direction: South
Element: Earth
Creature: 4-Legged Creatures
Human Resource: Love
Kind of Meditation: Lying
Way of Living: Right Speech
Four-Fold Way: Pay Attention
Healing Salve: Story-Telling
Instrument: Drum
Season: Spring

Cross-culturally, there are many different perspectives from the indigenous peoples of each continent regarding the directions and seasons. However, the majority view them as presented here.

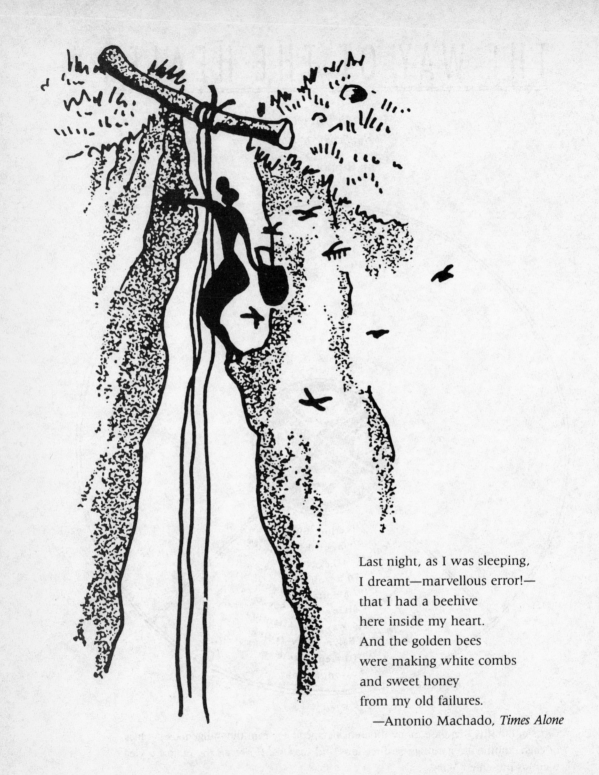

Last night, as I was sleeping,
I dreamt—marvellous error!—
that I had a beehive
here inside my heart.
And the golden bees
were making white combs
and sweet honey
from my old failures.
—Antonio Machado, *Times Alone*

PAY ATTENTION TO WHAT HAS HEART AND MEANING

The archetype of the Healer is a universal mythic structure that all human beings experience. Among indigenous cultures the Healer supports the principle of *paying attention to what has heart and meaning.* Healers in all major traditions recognize that the *power of love* is the most potent healing force available to all human beings. Effective Healers from any culture are those who extend the arms of love: acknowledgment, acceptance, recognition, validation, and gratitude.

People the world over consistently acknowledge each other in four ways: We acknowledge each other's skills; each other's character qualities; each other's appearance; and the impact we make on each other. Wherever we receive the least acknowledgment is where we may carry a belief of inadequacy or low self-esteem.

Healers in any tradition are inherently skilled in the art of acknowledgment. They fully recognize that the greatest remorse is love unexpressed. Probably the most powerful contemporary example of a person who demonstrates the healing power of extending love is Mother Teresa. In shamanic traditions she would be called a medicine woman.

The Four-Chambered Heart

Many native cultures believe that the heart is the bridge between Father Sky and Mother Earth. For these traditions the *four-chambered heart*, the source for sustaining emotional and spiritual health, is described as being full, open, clear, and strong. These traditions feel that it is important to check the condition of the four-chambered heart daily, asking: "Am I full-hearted, open-hearted, clear-hearted, and strong-hearted?"

Where we are not full-hearted, we approach people and situations half-heartedly. The experience of feeling like we should do something when we don't want to is the breeding ground for half-heartedness. Feeling half-hearted is an announcement of wrong placement, and it is time to remove ourselves from these situations.

Where we are not open-hearted, we become closed-hearted. Being defensive, encountering our own resistance, and protecting ourselves from the possibility of hurt are signals of closed-heartedness. The answer is to soften and reopen the heart.

Where we are not clear-hearted we are confused and carrying a doubting heart. This is where we need to wait. States of ambivalence and indifference are precursors to confusion and doubt. When we experience any of these states, we are reminded to wait for clarity rather than to take action.

Where we are not strong-hearted is where we lack the courage to be authentic or to say what is true for us. Strongheartedness is where we have the courage to be all of who we are in our life. The word "courage" is derived from the French word for heart, *coeur*, and etymologically it means "the ability to stand by one's heart or to stand by one's core." Whenever we exhibit courage, we demonstrate the healing power of paying attention to what has heart and meaning for us. As evidenced by the following Aztec poem, the combination of heart and its relationship to authenticity has been a perennial theme used throughout the ages.

> The mature person:
> heart firm as a stone,
> heart as strong as
> the trunk of a tree.
> Noble face, wise face;
> owner of his/her face
> owner of his/her heart.
> The mature person:
> noble face, firm heart.

The Six Kinds of Universal Love

Maintaining the health of our four-chambered heart allows us to explore and open to the six kinds of universal love:

1. Love between mates and lovers

2. Love between parent and child

3. Love between colleagues and friends

4. Professional love between teacher and student, therapist and client, and so on

5. Love of self

6. Unconditional love or spiritual love

Eight Concepts of Healing

All these kinds of love are doorways to healing. As we open to them, our ability to retain a balanced view of healing increases. Jeanne Achterberg, in her book *Woman as Healer*, reminds us of the following concepts, which contribute toward a balanced view of healing:

1. Healing is a lifelong journey toward wholeness.

2. Healing is remembering what has been forgotten about connection, and unity and interdependence among all things living and nonliving.

3. Healing is embracing what is most feared.

4. Healing is opening what has been closed, softening what has hardened into obstruction.

5. Healing is entering into the transcendent, timeless moment when one experiences the divine.

6. Healing is creativity and passion and love.

7. Healing is seeking and expressing self in its fullness, its light and shadow, its male and female.

8. Healing is learning to trust life.

When we are underdeveloped in any of these concepts, we find a closed door to love and health.

The Principle of Reciprocity

Healing involves the *principle of reciprocity*, the ability to equally give and receive and the ability to connect. Achterberg's eight concepts all reveal the principle of reciprocity at work. In order to maintain health and well-being, we need to maintain the balance between growing and receiving and to recognize when one mode is overextended and the other is under-expressed.

Many indigenous peoples would see Achterberg's concepts as ways human beings can stay in right relationship to Nature, and as a result stay in right relationship to their own nature. The principle of reciprocity monitors the balance of our health and love nature. Octavio Paz, in *The Labyrinth of Solitude*, puts it well:

> Love is one of the clearest examples of that double instinct which causes us to dig deeper into our own selves

Love consists in this, that two solitudes protect and touch and greet each other.
—Rainer Maria Rilke,
Selected Poetry

and, at the same time, to emerge from ourselves and to realize ourselves in another: death and re-creation, solitude and
communion.

EMPOWERMENT TOOLS OF THE HEALER

The empowerment tools of the Healer include the *four universal healing salves, journey work and the drum, lying meditation,*
and *cradling work.*

The Four Universal Healing Salves

Every culture has ways of maintaining health and well-
being. Healers throughout the world recognize the importance of maintaining or retrieving the four universal healing
salves: *storytelling, singing, dancing, and silence.* Shamanic societies believe that when we stop singing, stop dancing, are no
longer enchanted by stories, or become uncomfortable with
silence, we experience soul loss, which opens the door to
discomfort and disease. The gifted Healer restores the soul
through use of the healing salves.

It has long been recognized that these healing salves re-
awaken and sustain the divine child within us and return to
us the qualities of wonder, hope, and awe. Margaret Mead
described the natural function of these healing salves in

Women of Faith and Spirit (Warner and Beilenson) this way: "Prayer does not use any artificial energy, it doesn't burn up any fossil fuel, it doesn't pollute. Neither does song, neither does love, neither does the dance." Some native peoples add to Mead's statement when they say, "The Great Spirit must have loved stories, because he made a lot of people."

Storytelling

Native cultures transmit their values, ethics, and spiritual beliefs through songs, dances, silent rituals, prayer, and *storytelling*. As Peggy Beck and Anna Walters state in their book *The Sacred:*

> Human memory is a great storehouse which we ordinarily fill with only a fraction of its capacity. The elders knew this and tested and trained the memory along with the other senses, so that the history and traditions of the People could be preserved and passed on. One of the most important of the oral traditions was storytelling and the preservation of the origin histories.

Recent research by Joanne Martin and her team at Stanford Business School makes it clear that illustrative stories told within organizations encourage more commitment, generate more belief, and are more remembered than statistical data that "proves" the same point in a factual way. Even the impressionist painter Degas was adamant about this concept, as related by Barbara Shapiro in *Edgar Degas:* "It's all very well to copy what you see, but it is better to draw only what you see in memory. Then you reproduce only what has struck you, that is to say, the essentials. . . ." These essentials are the basis of all stories and ultimately shape our own life story.

Indigenous cultures recognize that storytelling can reshape an individual's experience or life story. Many shamans and medicine people are gifted storytellers. Such people are called "shape-shifters," because they have the capacity to shift the shape of an individual's story, or even to shift the shape of their own physical appearance. A shaman who has this ability is considered a healing catalyst and change agent. Contemporary shape-shifters are the gifted medical people, therapists, ministers, counselors, and others who assist people through life transitions.

The capacity to attend to our own life story permits us to reopen the heart and connect to the other universal healing salves. This in turn allows us to experience the human resource of love, the most powerful healing force on Mother Earth.

Journey Work and the Drum

Attending to our life story is a way of paying attention to what has heart and meaning. The Healer's way of listening to the heart is through *journey work*, a shamanic practice used to access information from the divine or sacred self and implemented in contemporary times by Michael Harner and the Foundation for Shamanic Studies. In journey work shamanic traditions surrender to the wisdom of the heart

Write the wrongs that are done to you in sand, but write the good things that happen to you on a piece of marble. Let go of all emotions such as resentment and retaliation, which diminish you, and hold onto the emotions, such as gratitude and joy, which increase you.

—Arabic proverb
(Van Ekeren, *The Speaker's Sourcebook*)

by doing lying meditation (see p. 58) to the accompaniment of the *drum* for approximately twenty to thirty minutes.

A natural altered state of consciousness is entered through the medium of *sonic driving* (rapid beating of the drum, usually four to seven cycles per second). If the drum is not used alone or with other drums, it may be accompanied by other instruments, such as the rattle, the bell, clicking of sticks or bones, and singing or chanting. Some indigenous peoples use this drumming practice to connect with healing and spiritual guidance. When we embark on such a journey, we open ourselves to the possibility of removing the blocks and obstacles to receiving love and giving love. This is the practice for developing a full, strong, open, and clear heart.

The drum is humankind's imitation of the heartbeat. Shamanic societies use the drum to facilitate healing and to sustain open-heartedness. In his research Andrew Neher reports that the sonic driving of the drum can affect the alignment of brain-resonant frequency with external auditory stimuli, and that this alignment can rebalance the central nervous system.

In Mickey Hart's book *Drumming at the Edge of Magic,* Nigerian drummer Babatunde Olatunji describes the inherent power of the drum's capacity to create realignment within the human system: "Where I come from we say that rhythm is the soul of life, because the whole universe revolves around rhythm, and when we get out of rhythm, that's when we get into trouble. For this reason the drum,

It is love that reveals to us the eternal in us and in our neighbors.
—Miguel de Unamuno,
Tragic Sense of Life

next to the human voice, is our most important instrument. It is special."

Melinda Maxfield furthers Neher's work and reinforces Olatunji's inherent knowing. Her research found that percussion in general and rhythmic drumming in particular facilitates imagery that is ritualistic and ceremonial in content. Maxfield's research reinforces the conclusion that journey work, combined with the sonic driving of the drum, accesses the psychomythology, or imagery and memory work, within each person which can support healing and help transform pathology. The journey/drum combination may be an ancient form of what we know today as a stress-reduction technique as well as a way of inducing a natural altered state. (See Appendix E for Maxfield's summary of her work.)

Lying Meditation

The *lying posture* is the most healing posture that the body can assume. The body equates this posture with rest and the nourishment that comes from receiving and giving love. It is the posture of surrender and openness. The lying posture assumed in the journey is a way of placing the body in its own "spirit canoe" in order to open to guidance and to receive healing. This provides us with an opportunity to observe both positive and challenging experiences that we need to address. The lying posture is used in many different cultures as the major posture in which to receive healing.

Every journey is considered sacred. The individual is required only to observe what is revealed in terms of feelings, sensations, memories, associations, visuals, sounds, smells, and nothingness. The sacred is honored by observing and remembering the material revealed during the journey. Many shamanic societies believe that while we are in our spirit canoe, the Great Spirit, the ancestors, and helping allies reveal to us what is needed for our current healing and guidance. One practice in the journey is to pay attention to where we go or to what is revealed. In this way we honor our own *psychomythology*, which holds the healing component for our own pathology.

The psyche is composed of three parts: *logos,* our inherent wisdom; *eros,* our love nature; and *mythos,* our life dream or myth. Reclaiming our personal psychomythology is the process of recalling and remembering our inherent wisdom and love nature through our life dream or mythos. Through image and journey work, the psyche will reflect back to us the guidance or healing work we need. Recurring dreams or favorite images are often our psyche's way of showing us what is important within our own nature. For example, if we dream repeatedly of going to school and taking exams, this may be an important message for us to pay attention to the repeated challenges or tests we are facing in our current life situations.

According to Brugh Joy, M.D., it takes approximately 13 billion brain cells to fire off one image or memory. It is important to pay attention to why a particular memory, association, or dream image is revealed at this time. If we

A religious awakening which does not awaken the sleeper to love has aroused him in vain.
—Jessamyn West
(Warner, *Women of Faith*)

devalue or discount what is shown to us in journey work, we disempower the creative force of our own psychomythology. The psyche is relentless about using every possible symbol, feeling, sensation, or memory to let us know where we are in our journey—physically, emotionally, mentally, and spiritually.

In shamanic societies symbols are the bridge between visible and invisible reality and are the psychological mechanisms for transforming energy. These traditions believe that our own symbolic structures contain divine revelations. Journeys are seen as teaching tools that provide healing, teaching, and visions. Each person is presented with what is spiritually needed. The journey may not include any of the experiences anticipated by the ego and its agenda, but the journey will always reveal the actual spiritual work desired within the individual's inherent psychomythology. Consequently, it is important to trust the psyche's wisdom and simply observe what is revealed during the journey, not to direct or control the process. Shamanic traditions hold that if nothing occurs within the journey, this is a time of waiting and integration rather than a time of taking action; or, taken literally, this is a time to do nothing.

In shamanic tradition there are three worlds that we may visit during a journey: the upper world, the lower world, and the middle world. All cultures have ascendancy and descendancy myths. Ascendancy myths are ultimately stories about journeys to the *upper world*, where we find magical places, important teachers, and experiences of upliftment and expansion. Journeys to the upper world are often symbolized by visiting gardens, flying on the back of birds, or meeting people who are important in our lives. In the upper world we receive guidance and healing.

Descendancy myths are stories about journeys to the *underworld*, where helping allies and power animals empower us to face our internal and external tests and challenges with courage. Journeys to the underworld—venturing into caves, going down to the bottoms of lakes, or traveling through tunnels—are ways that we retrieve lost parts of ourselves.

The *middle world* is what we call reality—the external world of health, finances, work, creativity, and relationships. When we find ourselves coming back to the room where we are taking the journey, we are being asked by our own psychomythology to bring our medicine or power into our life.

In a single journey, we may visit all three worlds or just one world. Wherever we go in a journey is where we will find what we need to become a healing agent and change master in our lives.

Cradling Work

Some shamanic traditions in parts of Africa and the Oceanic societies attend to health and well-being through what is called *cradling work*, a four-part practice in staying connected to the good, true, and beautiful aspects of one's nature. In cradling work we lie on our back and place both hands over our heart (in many cultures hands symbolize healing). Silently, we acknowledge the character qualities

All that is necessary to make this world a better place to live is to love—to love as Christ loved, as Buddha loved.
—Isadora Duncan
(Warner, *Women of Faith*)

that we appreciate about ourselves, we acknowledge our strengths, we acknowledge the contributions that have been made and continue to be made, and we acknowledge the love given and the love received.

In those societies mentioned above, this practice is generally done three times a day: once in the soft time of the day, morning; once in the strong time of the day, afternoon; and once in the subtle time of the day, night. Cradling work and the different times of day remind us that we are soft, strong, and subtle creatures. Today, this kind of healing work is called creative visualization, affirmation, or self-esteem work.

Cradling work and journey work, as we have seen, are forms of lying meditation. Forms of lying meditation are found in many spiritual traditions, and are used to access the human resource of love. It is the best posture in which to embrace and transform issues surrounding fear, anger, and control. It is also used to reopen oneself to the many arms of love, and rebalance the four-chambered heart.

THE HEALER'S CONNECTION TO NATURE

Native peoples recognize that the most empowering and healing tool we have available to us is our connection to nature and the wilderness. Many indigenous cultures refer to trees as "the medicine people of the plant kingdom," and shamanic societies become disturbed when large masses of trees are logged and not replanted. Indigenous peoples recognize that trees are important to the survival of all living creatures, and so regard them as having big medicine. Cross-culturally, trees are planted at births, marriages, deaths, and important initiations.

In many cultures trees symbolize transformation because of their ability to change form from season to season. The Bantu tribes of Africa have a Spring ceremony, in which they offer personal, traumatic wounds to a tree for healing purposes, with the intent never to speak out loud about that wound again. In the prehistoric societies of Europe, cave art reveals the same ritual, which is expressed by the hand-tree motif.

Indigenous peoples throughout the world recognize the connection between nature and healing. Saint Hildegarde of Bingen, a twelfth-century mystic, described the need for this interconnected relationship (in Fox, *Original Blessing*) when she said, "All nature is at the disposal of humankind. We are to work with it. For without it, we cannot survive." And a poem by an anonymous author says,

> Ancient tree seized
> A deep old reopened wound
> Timeless healing comes.

Other nature metaphors and symbols that are attributed to the way of the Healer include *Mother Nature* in its entirety.

With a stout heart, a mouse can lift an elephant.
—Tibetan proverb
(Feldman, *A World Treasury*)

Among many shamanic traditions, the direction of the *South* is associated with Mother Nature, the plant kingdom, the mineral kingdom, and all the *four-legged creatures.* This direction on the medicine wheel is where native peoples call forward the necessary people, rituals, and ceremonies for healing work.

The South is often associated with the season of *Spring;* therefore this direction and season is seen as the place for renewal, regeneration, and maintenance of health for many indigenous peoples. It is the direction for sustaining the health of the four-chambered heart, remembering the healing power found in the universal kinds of love, and carrying a balanced view of health. In this direction we can heal our woundedness and liberate the human resources caught in the shadow aspects of the healing archetype.

How the Unclaimed Healer Reveals Itself: The Shadow Aspects of the Healer Archetype, the Wounded Child of the South

We experience the shadow side of the Healer when we do not attend to our own health and well-being. To attend to our own health care requires a commitment to life-affirming patterns. When life-affirming patterns are not consistently present, the shadow side of this archetype is revealed by the wounded child of the South, who exhibits patterns of neediness and withdrawal and grows up to be the *martyr*. The Healer archetype may carry the shadow aspect, which reveals our own addictive nature and life-negating patterns. We often refer to these life-negating patterns as *addictions*. Underneath every addiction may well be an individual who is an indulgent martyr, unwilling to claim his or her health and well-being. Reinforcing life-negating patterns opens the doors to disease and discomfort.

Four Universal Addictions

Perhaps what we call individual addictions, such as to drugs, alcohol, and sex, are actually symptoms of deeper patterns of addiction that we share as a species. In looking at addictions from a cross-cultural perspective, I discovered that this is true and that there are four basic addictive patterns that human beings share:

1. The addiction to intensity. The unclaimed human resource is the expression of love.

2. The addiction to perfection. The unclaimed human resource is the expression of excellence and right use of power.

3. The addiction to the need to know. The unclaimed human resource is the expression of wisdom.

4. The addiction to being fixated on what's not working rather than what is working. The unclaimed human resource is the expression of vision and ways of looking at the whole.

The *addiction to intensity* is often demonstrated by individuals who have a low tolerance for boredom. If things become too dull or too routine, people who are addicted to intensity will dramatize, sensationalize, and exaggerate their life experience in order to feel alive. Many of these people will move to drugs, alcohol, and sex to intensify their experience and create the illusion of more vitality and aliveness. Intensity is the shadow side of love. If the addiction to intensity is well developed, waiting to be claimed is the human resource of love and the passionate four-chambered heart.

The *addiction to perfection* is the second addiction. Some indigenous societies clearly see the difference between per-

Tell me whom you love, and I'll tell you who you are.
—African-American proverb (Feldman, *A World Treasury*)

fection and excellence. Perfection does not tolerate mistakes, whereas excellence incorporates and learns from mistakes. People who have an addiction to perfection have little tolerance for mistakes or exposure of vulnerability of any kind. They equate vulnerability with weakness rather than strength. Contrary to this view, indigenous societies see the expression of vulnerability as an expression of strength. They inherently understand that vulnerability springs from the authentic self. Wherever we are addicted to perfection, we begin to walk the procession of the living dead or become like a walking mannequin. We deny our humanness and invest all our energy in maintaining a cultivated image or facade of how we want to be seen rather than exposing who we are. Perfection is the shadow side of excellence and the right use of power. If this addiction is well developed, waiting on the other side to be claimed is the human resource of power and excellent leadership skills.

The *addiction to the need to know* is the third addiction shared by humankind. It is important to inform oneself and to know things; yet in this addiction one is driven and compulsive about the need to know or the need to understand. These individuals do not like surprises or unexpected events. Where we are addicted to the need to know, we become masters of control and have strong trust issues. Everything needs to be compartmentalized, information needs to be controlled, and relationships need to be strategized. We become dogmatic, righteous, critical, and arrogant. These characteristics are the shadow side of wisdom.

If this addiction is well developed, the human resource of wisdom is waiting to be claimed. Wisdom includes the characteristics of objectivity, clarity, and discernment.

The *addiction of being fixated on what is not working* instead of what is working is the fourth addiction. The truth is that the majority of our life, when we look at it as a whole, is working. It is only a portion or a big slice of life that isn't working, but not the whole. If this addiction is well developed, there is a tendency to magnify negative experiences and blow them out of proportion. We tend to look at life from a fixed perspective, we don't recognize our blind spots, and we are unable to trust intuitive information. This addiction is the shadow side of the four ways of seeing: intuition, insight, perception, and vision. The four ways of seeing allow us to fully claim the gift of vision and release the addiction to being fixated on what is not working. When this addiction is fully disengaged, we begin to look at the blessings, gifts, talents, and resources that are available to us in our lives.

The Eight Universal Healing Principles

Eight healing principles, used in the majority of cultures, sustain health and well-being. When we do not fully attend to these principles we find ourselves on the shadow side of the Healer archetype. Study the chart below, and assess for yourself where you are supporting your health and well-being and where you are not attending to health-care issues.

Rebalancing those areas that are not supportive to our health and well-being allows us to fully reclaim the inner Healer.

SUPPORTS HEALTH AND WELL-BEING	NON-SUPPORTIVE OF HEALTH AND WELL-BEING
1. Balanced diet	1. Unbalanced diet
2. Daily and weekly exercise	2. Lack of exercise
3. Time for fun, play, and laughter	3. Loss of humor and lack of fun and play
4. Music, sonics, and chanting	4. Lack of music, sonics, and chanting
5. Love, touch, and support systems	5. Lack of touch, love, and support systems
6. Engaged in interests, hobbies, and creative purpose	6. Lack of interest, hobbies, and creative purpose
7. Nature, beauty, and healing environments	7. Lack of nature, beauty, and healing environments
8. The presence of faith and belief in the supernatural	8. Lack of faith and belief in the supernatural

PROCESSES AND REMINDERS: IMPORTANT PRACTICES TO DEVELOP THE INNER HEALER

1. *Spend at least fifteen minutes each day in lying meditation.* Record your experience in your journal or create a special meditation log.

Lying Meditation

Accessing the Inner Healer
Accessing the Quality of Love and Renewal

Purpose

The purpose of lying meditation is to honor sacred time. This is a time set aside for introspection, contemplation, discovery, and honoring the sacred or divine.

Posture

Lie on the floor with your eyes open and softly focused on a distant point. Put your arms at your side, with one resting parallel to your body and the other bent at the elbow with your forearm perpendicular to the floor. Having one arm raised will prevent you from going to sleep; should you fall asleep, your arm will awaken you when it falls to the floor or onto your body.

Process

Within this sacred time and posture you can consciously choose to heal yourself or others. You can get in touch with the healing, nurturing, loving, and caring energy inside you, and ask for divine guidance and assistance in healing wounded parts of your nature.

Lying meditation is the posture that is most associated with replenishment and the direct experience of human love and divine love. It is universally the posture that all human beings use for rest, sleeping, and dreaming. Used consciously, this posture can be a vehicle for building self-esteem and nurturing yourself in equal proportion to how you nurture others.

2. *Spend five to ten minutes doing cradling work as a way to sustain and increase self-esteem.*

The shamanic cradling exercise is a four-fold practice of honoring the greater being that you are, and remembering the cradle of interconnectedness that supports and binds all beings together.

Lie down in the posture of the inner Healer: Place your right hand over your heart, and your left hand over your right hand.

Then:

acknowledge your strengths and talents

acknowledge what character qualities you like about yourself

acknowledge the contributions that you have made and are making

acknowledge the love given and the love received

3. *Identify your wound—the story you always share about yourself that is tied to some traumatic event.* Offer this wound to a special tree, and never speak of this wound again. Some indigenous cultures use this practice as a way of making a commitment to healing the wounded part of ourselves.

The heart at rest sees a feast in everything.
—Hindi (Asian Indian) proverb (Feldman, *A World Treasury*)

4. *At least once a month, take a journey accompanied by the drum.* Use either a Michael Harner or *I Ching* drumming tape (see the bibliography for more information), or have someone drum for you.

5. *Spend some time each day checking the condition of your own four-chambered heart.* Are you paying attention to what has heart and meaning for you? Or is your heart entrapped by "shoulds"?

Medicine Man's Prayer

Listen, my dream!
This you told me should be done.
This you said should be the way.
You said it would cure the sick.
Help me now.
Do not lie to me.
Help me, Sun person.
Help me to cure this sick man.
—Blackfeet, in Bierhorst,
The Sacred Path

Summary of the Healer Archetype

The Healer archetype asks that we pay attention to what has heart and meaning. We develop our inner Healer when we attend to the condition and well-being of the four-chambered heart; when we extend acknowledgment and the arms of love to ourselves and others; and when we hold a balanced view of health.

Four-Chambered Heart

- The full heart
- The open heart
- The clear heart
- The strong heart

Four-chambered heart allows us to experience the six universal kinds of love

- Love between mates and lovers
- Love between parent and child
- Love between friends and colleagues
- Love between professional alliances; teachers/student; therapist/client; etc.
- Love of self
- Unconditional or spiritual love

Four Universal Categories for Human Acknowledgment

- Skills
- Character
- Appearance
- Impact that we have made upon another

The Arms of Love

- Acknowledgment
- Gratitude
- Validation
- Acceptance
- Recognition

FOUR HEALING SALVES: STORYTELLING SINGING DANCING SILENCE

Four Human Addictions and Human Resources Waiting to be Claimed

- Addiction to intensity (human resource: love)
- Addiction to perfection (human resource: power and excellence)
- Addiction to the need to know (human resource: wisdom)
- Addiction to what is not working, rather than what is working (human resource: vision)

Cradling Work

- Acknowledge your strengths
- Acknowledge the qualities that you like about yourself
- Acknowledge the contributions you are making and that you have made
- Acknowledge the love you have given and received and the love you are giving and receiving

Questions

Think about your responses to the following questions. To develop the inner Healer, ask and answer question 10 daily.

1. *What are my favorite childhood stories? What stories from childhood have I passed onto others?*

2. *What are the stories about myself that I bring forward when I meet new people?* What are your favorite spiritual stories, family stories, and love stories?

3. *What do I know about love? Who are the people that have been teachers of my heart?* Create a picture collage of your favorite teachers of the heart or write letters of gratitude to them.

4. *What are the blocks and obstacles that get in the way of my giving love? What are the blocks and obstacles that get in the way of my receiving love?*

5. *Where and with whom do I feel that my love is received? Who are the healing catalysts in my life?*

6. *Of the four universal acknowledgments, which have I consistently received? Which do I seldom receive?* (See Summary Chart.)

7. *Of the four addictions, where do I have the most experience and which is the most developed in me?* (See Summary Chart.)

8. *Review Jeanne Achterberg's balanced view of healing. Which of those concepts or views are not fully engaged or held in my own concept of healing? How can I incorporate these views into my daily life?*

9. *Of the eight universals that sustain health and well-being, which ones are currently over-expressed and which are undeveloped within my nature?* Use the rest of the year to bring all eight into balance.

10. *What is the condition of my four-chambered-heart: Where am I full-hearted? Where am I clear-hearted? Where am I open-hearted? Where am I strong-hearted?*

〰〰〰〰〰

AN ODE TO MY FATHER
HEALING THE CRITIC

When I awake in the morning,
It is either the very next day
after many, many days,
Or it is the very first day.
When it is the very next day
after many, many days,
I know the time has come
For me to walk through the door,
To take a look at that dark part of me
that is calling.
And to touch that place of willingness
to look again.
I know the time has come
For me to walk through the door

To take a look at this critic within,
Who only wants me to listen
To what needs to be heard,
So I then can heal
and bring that part of me
back to me.
When I awake in the morning,
It is either the very next day
after many, many days
Or it is the very first day.
Today, it is the very first day
Of what exists now.

—Twainhart Hill

THE WAY OF THE VISIONARY

*One of the things that little children do first is to sing and chant to
themselves. People spontaneously sing out of themselves—a different use
of voice. By ''song'' we don't have to limit ourselves to the idea of lyric
and melody, but should understand it as the voice as voice, which is
the Sanskrit goddess VAK—goddess of speech, music, language, and
intelligence. Voice itself is a manifestation of our inner being.*
—Gary Snyder, *The Real Work*

Direction: East
Element: Fire
Creature: Desert & No-Legged Creatures
Human Resource: Vision
Kind of Meditation: Walking
Way of Living: Right Placement
Four-Fold Way: Tell the Truth
Healing Salve: Singing
Instrument: Bell
Season: Summer

Cross-culturally, there are many different perspectives from the indigenous peoples
of each continent regarding the directions and seasons. However, the majority view them
as presented here.

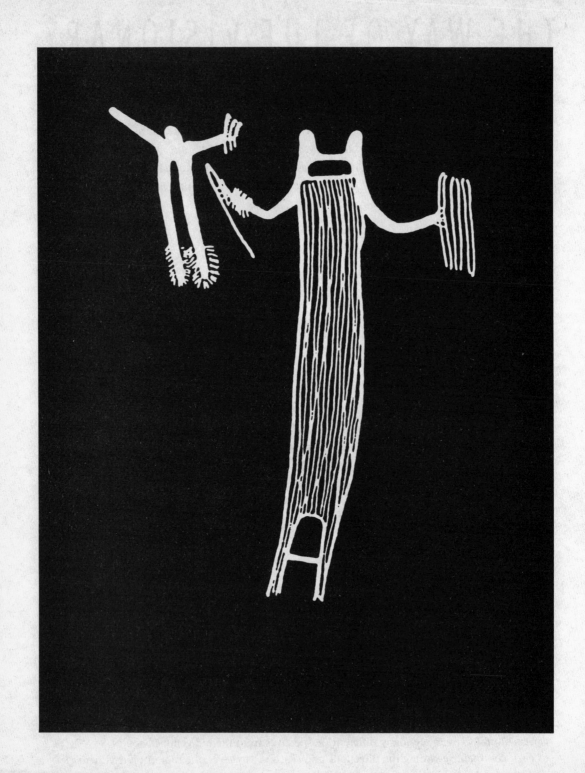

TELL THE TRUTH WITHOUT BLAME OR JUDGMENT

When we follow the way of the Visionary, we are able to make the truth visible. In indigenous societies visionaries may be shamans or artisans; but what is more important, these societies encourage all members to seek and express truth.

The principle that guides the Visionary is *telling the truth without blame or judgment*. When we express the inner Visionary, we know and communicate our *creative purpose and life dream*, act from our *authentic self*, are *truthful*, and *honor the four ways of seeing*.

Creative Purpose and Life Dream

All cultures respect the importance of vision and its capacity to magnetize, or open up, the creative spirit. The archetype of the Visionary is familiar to us all as that sometimes quiet but relentless reminder not to forget our life dream or purpose.

As was pointed out in the Way of the Warrior, many native cultures of the Americas hold a belief that each individual is original medicine, nowhere duplicated on the planet; therefore it is important to bring one's creative spirit, life dream, or purpose to earth. Not to do so precludes healing from coming into our family and our professional lives. Our work is to come fully forward with our gifts, talents, and resources, and to meet our tests and challenges. Gandhi recognized this simple truth when he said, "My life is my message."

Authenticity

When we remember who we are, we bring our authentic selves forward. Many times, however, we are forced at an early age to hide our true selves in order to survive. At some point this hiding becomes unnecessary, yet we find it hard to break the habit. Every day we choose anew whether we will support the authentic self or the false self.

Among some native cultures of the Americas, the term "Sacred Hoop" is synonymous with the term "authenticity," or being connected with one's spirituality. These peoples say that whenever we have the experience of being ourselves, we are "in our Sacred Hoop"; and when we have come home to who we are, we "sit inside our Sacred Hoop."

Ed McGaa, Eagle Man of the Oglala Sioux, reminds us in *Rainbow Tribe* of the power of ceremony and of returning home to self when he says, "The Great Mystery is obviously Truth. How close a people can come to the Creator's Harmony will decide the reach of the power within a ceremony."

THE FOUR-FOLD WAY

The majority of the spiritual traditions cite two patterns that can take us out of our Sacred Hoop, out of our true nature. Psychiatrist Roger Walsh in his book *Staying Alive* describes those patterns as the *patterns of denial* and the *patterns of indulgence.* Every human being, regardless of cultural conditioning and family imprinting, experiences these patterns at some time.

We express denial in our lives when we avoid certain people or issues and when we see things only as we want them to be rather than to accept them as they are. Underneath every denial pattern is the underlying fear that we will not be able to handle conflict and a deep human need to maintain peace, balance, and harmony at all costs. In deep denial we will abandon ourselves to keep the peace rather than communicate our feelings directly.

We express indulgence when we dramatize or sensationalize our experience. Often we exaggerate a situation or an issue in order to seek attention. Underneath this pattern is a high need for approval and acceptance that is ruled either by the fear of not being seen or the fear of being seen. People who make scenes, throw tantrums, or blow things out of proportion actually have a strong need for acceptance. Because they are terrified of their own feelings of insecurity or vulnerability, they use exaggeration as a way to hide those feelings.

It is the Visionary who knows how to dissolve the polarities and paradoxes that are found in patterns of denial and indulgence. The thirteenth-century Persian poet Rumi (in *Open Secret*, trans. by Barks) describes this process:

Out beyond ideas of wrongdoing and rightdoing,
there's a field,
I'll meet you there.

We can free the field of creativity that exists within each of us by moving out of ideas of wrongdoing or rightdoing. When we can answer "yes" to the question, "Is my self-worth as strong as my self-critic?" then we are ready to engage our creative expression beyond patterns of denial or indulgence. Rumi suggests that the field of unlimited creativity is always available when we are connected to our authenticity.

Truth-Telling

It is the Visionary's way to maintain authenticity and stay within the Sacred Hoop by telling the truth without blame or judgment. *Truth-telling* is a universal value that collapses patterns of denial and indulgence. Leslie Gray, from Oneida, Powattan, and Seminole lineage, who bridges the disciplines of Native Ethnic studies and psychology, says that in some native cultures, speaking the truth is called "speaking with spirit tongue." Author William Schutz, in *The Truth Option*, states that communication of truth makes for interpersonal richness. To fully present ourselves to each other, "and to have the most satisfying human relations, we must be both aware and honest."

To tell the truth without blame or judgment is the capacity to say what is so. The following examples illustrate how

Because those who do not know how to weep do not know how to laugh either.
—Golda Meir (Van Ekeren, *The Speaker's Sourcebook*)

we can say what is so without abandoning our ideas or feelings. Each statement carries no blame or judgment, and each reflects ways to "speak with spirit tongue":

"I'm jealous and afraid of losing you."

"I feel so judgmental and critical right now that I don't trust what will come out of my mouth."

"I'm disappointed with this situation because I had unrealistic expectations."

"I'm feeling insecure right now and need your reassurance."

"I'm so angry and upset right now that I need to take space."

"I don't know where I stand with you."

"This mode of communication doesn't work for me."

"I'm really excited about this new job, but I need more clarification on these tasks."

Communication that carries integrity always considers timing and context before the delivery of content. So often we know exactly what we want to say, but we do not consider whether it is the right time or the right place in which to deliver the content of our communication. Direct communication—giving voice to what we see without blame or judgment—means we must consider the alignment of appropriate word choice, tone of voice, and body posture.

The Four Ways of Seeing

It is important to honor the *four ways of seeing: intuition, perception, insight, and vision.* Many indigenous cultures recognize that intuition is the source that sparks external seeing (perception); internal viewing (insight); and holistic seeing (vision). For these societies, paying attention to these modes of seeing is a way to honor the sacred. We extend respect to our own visionary processes when we give voice to what we see or sense. The Visionary archetype impels us to bring our voice and creativity into the world.

The human resource of vision (the internal archetype of the Visionary) opens the creative spirit and pulls our voice and authenticity into the world. In *The Courage to Create*, psychoanalyst Rollo May states what shamanic traditions have practiced for centuries: "If you do not express your own original ideas, if you do not listen to your own being, you will have betrayed yourself."

The Visionary archetype—the relentless power within us that constantly extends an invitation to be who we are —requires the expression of authenticity, vision, and creativity. Writer Gertrude Stein tapped this archetype when she told emerging writers of her time, "You have to know what you want to get. But when you know that, let it take you. And if it seems to take you off the track, don't hold back, because perhaps that is instinctively where you want to be. And if you hold back and try to be always where you have been before, you will go dry" (Fritz, *The Path of Least Resistance*).

Man is not a being who stands still, he is a being in the process of becoming. The more he enables himself to become, the more he fulfills his true mission.

—Rudolph Steiner
(Van Ekeren, *The Speaker's Sourcebook*)

EMPOWERMENT TOOLS OF THE VISIONARY

The empowerment tools of the Visionary include *singing; bell work; meditation, contemplation,* and *prayer;* and *vision quests.*

Singing: Power Songs

All cultures bring voice into the world through the healing salve of *singing*. Through songs, chants, and storytelling, native societies practice staying inside their Sacred Hoop. Some native traditions say that one way to stay connected to the Great Spirit is to "sing for your life." In Africa it is said that "If you can talk, you can sing; if you can walk, you can dance." Oceanic societies believe that if you want to know how to tell the truth, begin to sing. These ancient societies have long realized that singing is a healing resource.

Among indigenous cultures there is a belief that our favorite songs are our *power songs*. Consider your own favorite songs. They are connected to the creative aspects of who you are, and reveal important aspects of your own authenticity. It is also believed that the most powerful song is the one that you create with your own words and your own melody. Begin to create your own repetoire of original

I don't sing because I'm happy; I'm happy because I sing.
—William James (Van Ekeren, *The Speaker's Sourcebook*)

power songs. Watch how the themes of your own songs release more creativity and reveal what has meaning for you.

Working with the voice in any way, whether it be singing, chanting, sounding, or voice induction work, feeds the essence of who we are. Peggy Beck and Anna Walters, in their book *The Sacred*, impress upon us the relationship between songs and spirit by reminding us how native traditions view this relationship: "The [indigenous] People equate or associate song, language, and breath—saying that human life is closely connected with breathing, and breathing with singing, singing with prayer, prayer with long life—one of the great circles of creation."

Liturgical music reminds us that the three *sacred sounds* found in all sacred music are directly related to the three universal life forces: dynamism, magnetism, and integration. These three sacred sounds are EE, OH, and AH. The sound of EE is the way human beings work with the life force of dynamism; the sound of OH is the way human beings work with the life force of magnetism; and the sound of AH is the way human beings work with the life force of integration. We use *dynamism* (EE) to initiate or move experiences. It is the energy that is used for expansion and growth. We use *magnetism* (OH) for opening, receiving, and deepening our experiences. We use *integration* (AH) to apply, synthesize, and consolidate experience. These three life forces are the forces that are necessary for creative expression. In order to begin any creative project, the dynamic aspect of our nature must first generate the project. Our magnetic nature is the life force that pulls new opportunities toward us to

The soul is always beautiful,
The universe is duly in order,
every thing is in its place,
What has arrived is in its
place and what waits shall be
in its place.
— Walt Whitman,
Complete Poetry

THE FOUR-FOLD WAY

enhance and further the project. It is the integrative energy that synthesizes and produces the actual creative project or product.

Shamanic chanting, Tibetan overtone sounds, the vocalizations of Judaic cantors, and Gregorian chants are all examples of spiritual traditions working with the three sacred sounds for purposes of realigning the three life forces. Preverbally, all children experiment with these three sounds as ways of realigning their own energetic patterns of dynamism, magnetism, and integration.

Bell Work

In most cultures the musical instrument that is equated with spirituality or calling people together is the *bell*. Archetypally, the bell serves as a sonic voice calling us back to remember our authentic purpose or "calling." Cross-culturally, the bell is a way to connect us to the spiritual aspects of ourselves. In some shamanic traditions, people tie bells to their ankles and wrists to serve as a reminder to bring tribal dreams, visions, and prayers to Mother Earth. Tibetan bells, Hindu bells, Oriental gongs, African bells, and bell choirs are ways to reinforce life dreams, prayers, visions, and spiritual inspiration.

Meditation, Prayer, Contemplation

All cultures have ways of accessing the supernatural or spiritual aspects of human nature. Traditionally, these forms include prayer, contemplation, and meditative practices. These are gateways and opportunities for getting in touch with the greater being that we are. Meditation is an opportunity to discover, uncover, and recover aspects of ourselves. Meditation might be thought of as a three-doored portal: It accesses symbols, memories, and associations; it functions as a bridge between the outer and inner worlds; and it reveals the divine creature that we are. In indigenous cultures meditative practices are equated with journey work, through which native peoples honor the sacred. It is their way of attaining a naturally induced altered state or form of meditation or contemplation.

Walking Meditation

Through *walking meditation* our inner Visionary opens us to our creativity. In walking meditation we consciously choose an issue to focus on, let it go, then observe what is revealed to us while walking.

This form of meditation is sometimes referred to as "moving meditation." Whether walking, cooking, running, or swimming, we find ourselves in an altered state of consciousness or meditative mode. When our body is moving and open, we become vehicles for creative problem-solving.

Walking or moving meditation releases our creative spirit. It is important to pay attention to our processes or to the creative problem-solving that is occurring when we are involved in this type of meditation. Some indigenous cultures walk great distances during initiation rites as a way to reclaim the authentic self. These are known as "walk-abouts" among the Aboriginals of Australia, and as vision quests among the native peoples of North America. Their purpose is to instill creative resourcefulness in order to teach survival techniques and methodologies.

Power of Prayer

Prayer can be the vehicle for creatively visualizing desired experiences and outcomes. Larry Dossey, M.D., in *Recovering the Soul*, states that prayer has long been held by most religious traditions to contain potent healing power, and has a long and honored history as a form of intervention in illness. He says that "prayer researchers" and "scientist-clinicians" offer us some of the most remarkable evidence that the mind may indeed be non-local and can act on matter in decisive ways—ways that may make the difference between life and death for the sick person. "Our problems assessing the role of prayer in health come about in large measure because of the curious way we think about the concept of distance and locality in medicine." Many indigenous peoples recognize that through prayer, dreams, and visions, individuals can touch the heart and spirit of other human beings, regardless of physical time and distance.

For the Basque philosopher Miguel de Unamuno, prayer was a way of nurturing the hunger for divinity and connecting to the well-being found in human nature. In *Tragic Sense of Life*, he eloquently describes what happens when we connect to our own divinity: "This longing or hunger for

I pray and I sing. And sometimes my prayer is my singing.
—Bobby McFerrin

divinity begets hope, hope begets faith, and faith and hope beget charity. Of this divine longing is born our sense of beauty, of finality, of goodness."

In meditation we listen to and observe the guidance that is given. The distinction between prayer and meditation is best described by a nine-year-old friend who said, "Prayer is when you talk to God, and meditation is when you listen to what God has to say." In most societies prayer is a way to have a dialogue with the sacred. May Sarton echoes this definition in her *Journal of a Solitude,* when she relates Simone Weil's definition of prayer: "Absolute attention is Prayer."

Cross-culturally, attention to the sacred has created three kinds of prayers: petitionary prayers, prayers of worship, and prayers of gratitude. *Directed prayer,* often called petitionary prayer, is when we have a specific goal, image, or outcome in mind. *Nondirected prayer,* in contrast, involves an open-ended approach in which no specific outcome is held in mind. In nondirected prayer the individual does not attempt to tell the universe what to do. In Western terms the nondirected prayer often ends with the phrase, "Thy will be done" or, "For the highest good of all concerned." Both directed and nondirected forms of prayer can include prayers of worship and gratitude.

Some indigenous cultures use repetitive songs for prayer. They use both directed and nondirected prayer, because they consider dreams, visions, and insights as revelations or prayers that can be used for family members, friends, colleagues, and Mother Nature. Directed prayer involves intention, and nondirected prayer involves trust. Combining both allows us to fully access our vision and to connect to our own faith, and to trust the mystery of who we are.

Vision Quests

Many shamanic traditions hold the belief that any solitary time that is spent in nature for purposes of reflection and guidance reawakens us to our own life purpose and remembering the original medicine that is ours to offer to all creatures and human beings.

Much emphasis is given to demonstrating ways of trusting one's vision and intuition, especially in the *vision quest* context. Many indigenous cultures use the vision quest, an extended time of solitude spent in nature, for purposes of revisioning, reclaiming, and remembering one's life dream or creative spirit. Modern-day wilderness excursions, like backpacking, camping, hiking, and solitary retreats in nature, use vision quest principles to obtain similar results.

As children we spent more time outdoors than we did indoors. As adults we have a tendency to do the reverse. Inherently, the child within us instinctively knows that outer nature is a profound reflection and teacher of our own inner nature. Psychoanalyst Carl Jung became very depressed in mid-life. He recognized that in order to retrieve his own life dream or purpose, he would need to reclaim the divine child within. He began to reflect on his childhood, and remembered that he had always gone into a timeless space whenever he built sand castles out of small pebbles. As an adult he used this information to pull himself out of his depression, and acted on it by building his own home out of large stones and sand mortar.

As a result of this experience, Jung discovered that our life mythos, or dream, may very well be held in those childhood activities that we were drawn to do by ourselves, for hours. Often he would have his clients go back to the ages between four and twelve to remember those timeless solitary activities. In reclaiming these memories and activities, we are able to revitalize the quality of our life experience by bringing the divine child and life dream back into our adult activities.

THE VISIONARY'S CONNECTION TO NATURE

Speak to the earth,
and it shall teach thee.
  —Job 12:8

Some indigenous societies use the vision quest as a way to revision, redream, and review one's intention and whether it is aligned with creative purpose. Times in solitude, particularly connected to nature, allow us to renew and regenerate our own natures.

Among many shamanic traditions, the direction of the *East* is considered the home of the *rising sun,* the *Great Spirit, desert creatures, serpents, lizards,* and *turtles.* On the medicine wheel, this direction is the place where some native peoples call forward the power of vision, dreams, and spiritual guidance. The East is often associated with the season of *Summer;* therefore this direction and season is seen as the place of abundance, fullness, and prosperity. Summer is the season when nature comes into its fullness. Oracular traditions in every society are ways human beings have drawn upon the resource of vision to support coming into their full nature. This direction reminds us to connect to the mystery of who we are, to actualize the fullness of our life dream, and to give voice to what we see.

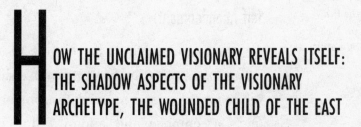

HOW THE UNCLAIMED VISIONARY REVEALS ITSELF: THE SHADOW ASPECTS OF THE VISIONARY ARCHETYPE, THE WOUNDED CHILD OF THE EAST

The Visionary archetype, as we have seen, is the truth-teller. We experience the shadow side of the Visionary whenever we deny our own truth, our authenticity. The three major mechanisms of self-denial are the *false-self system, self-abandonment,* and *projection.*

The False-Self System

We express the shadow side of the Visionary when we feed the *false-self system* rather than stay in our authenticity. Latin Americans have a folk saying (from Feldman, *A World*

Treasury) which describes the danger of holding onto the false-self, "Whoever has a tail of straw should not get close to the fire." We feed the false self and develop our "straw tails" by editing our thoughts, rehearsing our emotions, performing what we think people want to see, or hiding our true selves. We feed the false-self system whenever we are unwilling to tell the truth, say what is so, or give voice to what we see. Whenever we pretend, edit, rehearse, perform, or withhold, we support the development of the false-self system. Through the false self, we develop the art of self-abandonment.

Self-Abandonment

The major shadow aspect of the Visionary archetype is *self-abandonment*. Human beings universally abandon themselves for five major reasons: for someone's love; for someone's acceptance and approval; to keep the peace; to maintain balance; or to stay in the state of harmony. When we abandon ourselves for someone's love, pretending to be other than who we are in order to get someone's love, acceptance, or approval, it is a form of self-abandonment. Another way we abandon ourselves—in order to keep the peace, balance, and harmony—is to avoid difficult issues or by not saying what is actually so for us.

In some shamanic traditions, those who have abandoned themselves would be said to have difficulty "speaking with spirit tongue" and would be considered "weak-hearted" rather than "strong-hearted." The wounded child of the East is the covert, manipulative, deceptive child who is weak-hearted and grows up to be the strategist with the hidden agenda. Weak-heartedness is where we lack the courage to be who we are. Whenever we lack courage to be who we are, we move into self-abandonment.

If we are consistently involved in patterns of self-abandonment, our authentic self is waiting to be claimed. Through truth-telling we can collapse our self-abandonment patterns, begin to free ourselves from the false self, and release ourselves from the shadow side of the Visionary archetype. Relationships help us to see where we are able to stay inside our Sacred Hoop and maintain our authenticity, or where we feed the false-self system rather than maintaining our integrity.

Reflective Mirrors: Projections

Many indigenous cultures sew small pieces of reflective glass or mirrors into ceremonial costumes or glue them onto masks to remind us that we are mirrors for each other. The motif of the *mirror,* as a metaphor of reflection, is found cross-culturally. For some indigenous peoples, those who are mirrors for us become our teachers, and demonstrate ways that we may reclaim authenticity by speaking with spirit tongue.

These societies believe each person can be either a clear mirror, a smoking mirror, or a split mirror. *Clear mirrors* are individuals who we idealize or believe that we cannot be like; *smoking mirrors* are individuals with whom we have difficulty and hope that we are not like them in any way; and *split mirrors* are people who we like and admire, yet we experience fear or constriction in their presence.

The psychological term for these diverse kinds of mirrors is *projection.* We know a projection is at work when there is an energetic charge. Projections are unclaimed self-perceptions. Projections are parts of ourselves that are on their way home, yet are still disowned. We find it more comfortable to have these aspects outside of ourselves, rather than to embrace them as a part of who we are. When we express the Visionary archetype, we update our self-perceptions to accurately reflect the person we have become.

Some indigenous cultures recognize that the way of the Visionary is a method for staying connected to the authentic self and for revealing those parts of our nature that are caught in the shadow aspect of this archetype. The concept of the shadow actually means any part of ourselves, positive or challenging, that is not integrated or accepted within our nature. Those shadow parts of us will dominate or persist until they are integrated.

The Five Stages of Projection

In 1984, at a conference in San Francisco entitled "The Dark Side," poet Robert Bly synthesized psychoanalyst Maria von Franz's work on projection and Alice Miller's work on childhood, and presented the *five stages of projection.* Projections can be either positive or challenging. The positive aspect of

To look into a mirror;
And to be a mirror,
I find myself again.
  —Anonymous

every projection is that it is a disowned part of ourselves on its way home. Before we fully reclaim disowned parts of ourselves, it is necessary to go through the five stages of projection.

1. *We look around and find the perfect person to hold our projection.* For example, if we have not claimed our leadership or beauty, we will often idealize people with strong leadership skills or idealize someone who we see as beautiful. If we have difficulty expressing our anger, we will often have difficulty with someone who does express anger. This becomes a challenging projection for us. In this stage we never see people for who they are; we see only what we want them to be for us.

2. *The projection begins to slip.* We begin to see that the individual may be something other than what we have projected; however, we readjust the projection with rationalization and excuses because we don't want to believe this is part of our own nature. For example, the effective leader may have unskillfully handled a situation, yet we rationalize that everyone has a hard day or that the people involved actually deserved the treatment. By doing this, the projection that had begun to slip is put quickly back into place.

3. *The projection totally falls off.* No rationalizations can be made. We are forced to see who the person is beyond what we projected. In this stage we become disappointed, angry, blaming, and judgmental. Now we have the choice to either

move to stage four or to pick up the projection and look for another person to carry it for us rather than bring it home. Often we spend years just doing stages one, two, and three. We find different people to hold the same projection of those parts of ourselves that we are unwilling to bring home and claim. For example, if we find our own anger difficult to accept, we may often put it outside of ourselves, and judge or avoid it when we see it expressed in another person. Some indigenous societies would see this stage as the smoking mirror.

Truth may walk through the world unarmed.
—Bedouin proverb
(Feldman, *A World Treasury*)

4. *Recognition.* We realize that it was a projection, and we see that it was our own material. It is the *stage of grief:* grief for the lost part of ourselves that has been away for so long; and grief from the recognition that we didn't see the other person for who he or she was, and now recognize the unintentional harm that we may have done in stage three.

5. *Compassion for and integration of the projection.* In this stage we have compassion for ourselves and others with similar issues. We model the quality that we once projected rather than continue to place the projection outside of ourselves. We move into a state of objectivity and carry no charge one way or the other about what we had once projected.

When people are split mirrors for us, we are simultaneously drawn to them yet wary of them. The split mirror is the combination of both the clear and smoking mirrors. The five stages of projection would apply in the same way.

Fixed Perspectives/Blind Spots

Where we lose our capacity to play or to maintain our sense of humor, we find ourselves either seeing only that which is not working, or becoming attached to our own perception as the only viewpoint to have. In either case, whether it's our *blind spots* or *fixed perspectives*, we lack spontaneity and become over-identified with our own ways of looking at things.

Confucius said, "Beware of the man who laughs and his belly does not jiggle; that is a dangerous person." When we are not connected to our own integrity, we become dangerous. Real laughter, however, has the capacity to free us from the false-self system. Fixed perspectives, blind spots, and aligning to social protocol rather than aligning to our integrity signal that we are involved with the shadow aspects of the visionary archetype.

Humor, laughter, and forms of play are ways to open to alternative viewpoints. Ethel Barrymore's statement (from Van Ekeren, *The Speaker's Sourcebook*) reminds us of the magic that is created when laughter is connected with integrity: "You grow up the day you have your first real laugh—at yourself." If we maintain our sense of humor, spontaneity, and child-like curiosity, we are able to creatively use the four ways of seeing. We implicitly trust our perceptions, insights, dreams, and visions. Creative options and visions presented by others begin to inspire and stimulate our creativity when we are not caught by the shadow aspects of this archetype. Creative individuals are open to multiple ways of looking;

and they are very facile in letting go and moving toward options or perspectives they had not considered.

Processes and Reminders: Important Practices to Develop the Inner Visionary

1. *Spend at least fifteen minutes each day in walking meditation.* Record your experience in your journal or create a special meditation log.

Walking Meditation

Accessing the Inner Creator
Accessing the Quality of Creativity

Purpose

The purpose of walking meditation is to honor sacred time. This is a time set aside for introspection, contemplation, discovery, and honoring the sacred or divine.

Posture

Walk at a comfortable pace, and in a relaxed manner, for at least fifteen minutes. Many other movement activities can also be consciously used as meditation, including running, swimming, dancing, driving, cooking, vacuuming. In essence, any physical activity you choose for the purpose of listening to your internal states or processes can be considered a vehicle for meditation.

Process

This posture supports the aspects of trust and openness, and encourages the unexpected, because your attention is engaged in a moving activity. During these activities intuitive insights and creative solutions often appear spontaneously. Moving meditation teaches human beings about the wonder of what can happen when we trust and let go of control.

2. *Spend some time each day honoring your dreams by recording them in a dream journal.* The most important dreams to work with during the year are the ones you keep remembering.

3. *Make a commitment to practice truth-telling on a daily basis.* Notice with whom and in what situations this is easy for you and when it is challenging.

4. *Spend at least fifteen minutes each day singing, humming, or chanting.* Begin to create your own original power songs.

5. *Set aside some time each season to review your goals and how they support and further your life dream or vision.*

6. *At least twice a year, spend some extended time alone in nature to revision, redream, and reflect.*

7. *Consciously extend prayer or nonverbal support to others.* Use creative visualizations, affirmations, and visual reminders to support your own growth and development.

8. *Spend quiet time each day listening to your intuition.* Deep inner guidance is always available and waiting to be recognized and used.

9. *Notice and observe the sources of inspiration in your life.* They reveal what is important to the authentic self.

Someone who sees you and does not laugh
   out loud,
or fall silent, or explode in pieces,
is nothing more than the cement
and stone of his own prison.
   —Jalal al-Din Rumi

THE FOUR-FOLD WAY

Summary of the Visionary Archetype

The Visionary archetype asks us to tell the truth without blame or judgment. We express the Visionary when we honor the four ways of seeing and the power of prayer; when we give voice to what we see internally and externally; and when we bring forward our creative spirit and life dream.

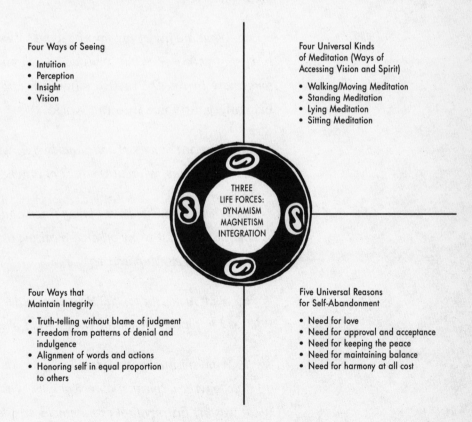

Four Ways of Seeing

- Intuition
- Perception
- Insight
- Vision

Four Universal Kinds of Meditation (Ways of Accessing Vision and Spirit)

- Walking/Moving Meditation
- Standing Meditation
- Lying Meditation
- Sitting Meditation

THREE
LIFE FORCES:
DYNAMISM
MAGNETISM
INTEGRATION

Four Ways that Maintain Integrity

- Truth-telling without blame of judgment
- Freedom from patterns of denial and indulgence
- Alignment of words and actions
- Honoring self in equal proportion to others

Five Universal Reasons for Self-Abandonment

- Need for love
- Need for approval and acceptance
- Need for keeping the peace
- Need for maintaining balance
- Need for harmony at all cost

Questions

Think about your responses to the following questions. To develop the inner Visionary, ask and answer questions 1 and 2 daily.

1. *What is my current capacity for truth-telling without blame or judgment?* Practice truth-telling, and notice each day those instances where you were able to express the truth without blame.

2. *In what situations and with what people do I find myself feeding the false-self?*

3. *What are five of my favorite songs? What songs from childhood stay with me? What songs do I teach others? What original songs have I created?* Practice singing every day as a way of bringing your voice into the world.

4. *Between the ages of four and twelve, what activities captivated me for hours, without the need of anyone else around?*

5. *Where in my life have I brought forward the creative aspects of who I am? What is my original medicine (my gifts and talents) that is nowhere else duplicated?*

6. *What makes me laugh? How developed is my sense of humor? What is fun for me? What are the forms of play in my life?*

7. *What spiritual paths, ideas, and practices have I engaged in? If I were to write a spiritual autobiography, what would it contain? What was my first mystical or numinous experience?*

8. *What forms of prayer, meditation, or contemplation do I use for guidance? Where do I look for guidance? What practices connect me to my inner life?*

9. *In what situations or with which people do I abandon myself? Where am I able to maintain my integrity and authenticity, and where am I not able to do so?*

10. *What projections am I aware of? Who are the clear mirrors, smoking mirrors, and split mirrors in my life?*

*each of us carries
in our chest
a song*

*so old
we don't know
if we learned it*

*some night
between the murmurs
of fallen kisses*

*our lips
surprise us
when we utter*

*this song
that is singing
and crying at once*
    —Francisco X Alarcon,
    Body in Flames

THE WAY OF THE TEACHER

*True mastery can be gained by letting things go their
own way. It can't be gained by interfering.*

—Lao Tzu, *Tao Te Ching* (Mitchell)

Direction: West
Element: Water
Creature: Water Creatures
Human Resource: Wisdom
Kind of Meditation: Sitting
Way of Living: Right Timing
Four-Fold Way: Open to Outcome
Healing Salve: Silence
Instrument: Sticks, Bones
Season: Autumn

Cross-culturally, there are many different perspectives from the indigenous peoples
of each continent regarding the directions and seasons. However, the majority view
them as presented here.

BE OPEN TO OUTCOME, NOT ATTACHED TO OUTCOME

The way of the Teacher accesses the human resource of wisdom, and every culture has traditional and nontraditional means of education. Whether it is an established school system or an apprenticeship, the process of learning and teaching is universal.

The principle that guides the Teacher is to be *open to outcome, not attached to outcome.* The Teacher has *wisdom,* teaches *trust,* and understands the need for *detachment.*

Wisdom: Clarity, Objectivity, Discernment, Detachment

The way of the Teacher is a practice in trust. *Trust* is the container out of which the *qualities of wisdom* grow: clarity, objectivity, discernment, and detachment. Wisdom is at work when we are open to all options.

It is the Teacher's way to use trust as an instrument. Mother Teresa demonstrated trust when she said: "I feel like a pencil in God's hands . . . God writes through us, and however imperfect instruments we may be, he writes beautifully . . . He deigns to work through us. Is that not marvelous?" (Warner, *Women of Faith*).

Trust: Being Comfortable with Uncertainty

Shamanic traditions access the human resource of wisdom by learning how to trust and to be comfortable with states of not knowing. In some parts of Africa, an individual who is in a place of not knowing is said to be "walking the land of gray clouds." During times of not knowing, it is considered foolish to take action and an act of wisdom to wait and trust. Trust, however, can be a difficult skill to learn.

The *trickster* archetype found in many shamanic traditions functions as a Teacher who shocks people into seeing their attachments and habitual patterns. Tricksters typically present surprises and the unexpected as a way of waking people out of their routines. In their book *Synchronicity: Science, Myth, and the Trickster*, Allan Combs and Mark Holland clearly describe this figure:

> In the mythologies of many peoples, the mythic figure who is the embodiment of the unexpected is the Trickster, who steps godlike through cracks and flaws in the ordered world of ordinary reality, bringing good luck and bad, profit and loss. The trickster god is universal. He is known to the Native American peoples as Ictinike, Coyote, Rabbit and others; he is Maui to the Polynesian Islanders; Loki to the old Germanic tribes of Europe; and Krishna in the sacred mythology of India. Best known to most of us in the West is the Greek god Hermes, who represents the most comprehensive and sophisticated manifestation of the Trickster. Homer calls Hermes the "Bringer of Luck." He is also known, in one of the many paradoxes that characterize Hermes and other trickster gods, as the patron of both travelers and thieves. He is the Guide of Souls to the underworld

Every head is a world.
—Cuban proverb
(Feldman, *A World Treasury*)

and messenger to the gods. As all these roles suggest, he is the quintessential master of boundaries and transitions. It is by this mastery that he surprises mundane reality with the unexpected and the miraculous.

The opposite of trusting in the unexpected is trying to *control* the uncontrollable—clearly an impossible task. Shamanic societies recognize that an individual who has difficulty with surprises or the unexpected has attachments, fixed perspectives, and a strong need for control. Attachments are specific, immovable expectations, desires that are projected onto people, places, and situations. When we are attached, we often become controlling and rigid. The trickster figure reminds us to become more resilient and objective.

From the unreal lead me to the real,
From darkness lead me to light
From death lead me to immortality.
—The Upanishads

The Theme of Detachment

The primary purpose of the trickster archetype is to teach human beings about detachment. Most Westerners equate the word "detachment" with "not caring." Linguistically, however, the word *detachment* is most often defined as "the capacity to care deeply from an objective place." So, when we use the term "detachment" here, we are speaking of what you may think of as nonattachment, letting go, maintaining our sense of humor. If we observe what causes us to lose our sense of humor, we can identify our point of attachment. Where we maintain our sense of humor is where we are detached and can remain flexible.

When we are detached, we are able to calmly observe our reactions to situations and not get pulled into an emotional position. Don't confuse this with coldness and not caring—it's quite the opposite. When we don't get pulled in, and when we maintain our sense of humor, we demonstrate our own capacity to care deeply from an objective place.

The majority of spiritual traditions address the theme of detachment. Harrison Owen, in his book *Leadership Is,* has consolidated these themes into four principles, which he calls the immutable laws of the spirit: "Whoever is present are the right people to be there; whenever we start, it's always the right time; what happens is the only thing that could have happened; when it's over, it's over." Underlying each of these premises, whether we agree with them or not, is the principle of acceptance rather than resignation. Can we accept the experience as it is and then be creative with it, rather than be resigned or fatalistic about it? Acceptance is an important part of detachment. The feeling of resignation is always a sign of the presence of attachment.

Loss and Ritual

Another way we learn about detachment is through *loss.* William Bridges, in his book *Surviving Corporate Transition,* says that losses characteristically fall into the following six categories:

1. Loss of attachments
2. Loss of turf

The dream begins with a teacher who believes in you, who tugs and pushes and leads you to the next plateau, sometimes poking you with a sharp stick called "truth."

—Dan Rather
(Van Ekeren, *The Speaker's Sourcebook*)

3. Loss of structure

4. Loss of a future

5. Loss of meaning

6. Loss of control

We have all experienced one or more of the losses Bridges mentions, plus the loss of loved ones. Each type of loss is a humbling experience that further teaches us about acceptance and letting go.

Many shamanic traditions recognize that *ritual* helps people deal with loss. Combs and Holland remind us that "the word ritual, in fact, comes from the Indo-European root which means 'to fit together.' It is related to such words as art, skill, order, weaving, and arithmetic, all of which involves fitting things together to create order." All societies have rituals to acknowledge the major life transitions of birth, initiation, marriage, and death. Ritual is the conscious act of recognizing a life change, and doing something to honor and support the change through the presence of such elements as witnesses, gift giving, ceremony, and sacred intention. In this way human beings support the changes they are experiencing and create a way "to fit things together again."

Death does not take the old but the ripe.
—Russian proverb
(Feldman, *A World Treasury*)

Ancestor Spirits

Some native traditions see *ancestor spirits* (family members and friends who are no longer living) as important teachers of detachment because they have faced the process of letting go and of experiencing the ultimate unknown, death. Indigenous peoples believe that these spirits literally stand behind us to support us in our life dream and purpose. The majority of shamanic traditions believe that the male ancestor spirits stand behind us on the right side of the body, and the female ancestor spirits stand behind us on the left side of the body. They believe that ancestor spirits are invested in seeing that the current generations and the generations to come fulfill their dreams or life purpose. This old European ancestral song, passed down through an oral tradition, clearly states how ancestors may support us:

> Oh, may this be the one who
>   will bring forward
> the good, true and beautiful in our
>   family lineage;
> Oh, may this be the one who will
>   break the harmful
> family patterns or harmful nation
> patterns.

Barrier Canyon, Utah

In *Tragic Sense of Life*, the Basque philosopher Miguel de Unamuno reminds us of the importance of ancestral connections and the help that is deeply rooted within us: "All my ancestors live undiminished in me and will continue so to live, united with me, in my descendants." Native societies of North America, in many of their prayers, remind us of this past and present connection when they say, "For the past generations and the seven generations to come, I pray for. . . ." Many indigenous cultures recognize that each individual is a tradition bearer for the past generations and for the generations to come. It is important to consider in what ways we can bring forward the "good, true, and beautiful" that is carried in our heritage; and to know that the quality of our life contributes to the opportunities and challenges for future generations to come. When we find ourselves thinking of favorite aunts or grandparents who are no longer alive, we may often be reminded of the good, true, and beautiful in our own nature.

Many indigenous societies believe that ancestor spirits are present to help us through the last doorway and the process of dying. Because ancestor spirits teach us about letting go and about detachment, they are Teachers who help us prepare for unknown and unfamiliar experiences, the greatest of which is our death.

Our reactions to the new experiences we meet daily may well be a preparation for how we will handle or approach our death. Do we approach new experiences with curiosity, wonder, or excitement? Or do we handle the unexpected and unfamiliar by becoming controlling and fearful? In considering the last utterances of important people as they approach the last doorway, we get a glimpse of how others handled letting go. Junípero Serra, the Spanish missionary, faced that last doorway by saying, "Now I shall rest." Gertrude Stein's last words were, "What is the question—if there is no question, there is no answer." Goethe approached his death by saying, "More light" (Conrad, *Famous Last Words*).

If we call upon the ancestor spirits for help in facing unfamiliar situations, we can also call on them for help in actualizing our life dream. Poet John Milton reminds us in *Paradise Lost* of the unlimited resource of our heritage and lineage that is honored through the ancestor spirits: "Millions of spiritual creatures walk the Earth / Unseen, both when we wake, and when we sleep. . . ." Many shamanic traditions classify Milton's "spiritual creatures" or ancestor spirits into three categories: ancestors who are our biological family; extended family and friends who are not blood related; or figures in history who are sources of inspiration. These societies consider blood family ancestors to be the most powerful ancestors for helping us to break harmful family patterns so that we can retain the good, true, and beautiful.

EMPOWERMENT TOOLS OF THE TEACHER

The empowerment tools of the Teacher archetype include observing *silence, calling the ancestor spirits* for guidance, and *sitting meditation.*

Silence

We can open to the Teacher archetype and the ancestor spirits through the healing salve of *silence.* Many spiritual traditions recognize that inner guidance and transpersonal experiences come forth during times of silence or extended periods of solitude. In order to tap the human resource of wisdom, it is necessary to practice the art of listening. As Mark Twain put it, "A better idea than my own is to listen" (Harnsberger, *Everyone's Mark Twain*).

Listening to our own guidance is a way of honoring our inherent wisdom. Periods of silence and solitude allow us to obtain more clarity, objectivity, and discernment, the qualities inherent to wisdom. Where we seek guidance, internally and externally, is where we are willing to learn and to listen.

An ancient source of guidance is the Chinese *Book of Changes*, known as the *I Ching*. This resource in its use of nature metaphors reminds us that in order for change to be successful, we must be like a great rooted tree by a flowing river. That is, we need to balance both quietude (the rooted tree) and activity (the flowing river), or stillness with movement. In the West we know almost too well the importance of activity and movement; we also need to understand that silence and periods of solitude are essential ways to open to inner guidance and to replenish our soul.

Calling the Ancestor Spirits

During periods of silence, we can also obtain guidance from ancestor spirits to help us with family challenges. Some shamanic traditions believe that calling the names of the ancestors will bring their help forward. Sometimes musical instruments are used in connection with the ancestor spirits.

The *clicking of sticks* or *bones* is another way to ask for ancestral help; each clicking sound represents our commitment to break harmful family patterns or harmful cultural patterns. In *Jambalaya*, Luisah Teish, of the Yoruba Lucumi tradition, reminds us that, "Africans believe that those who go before us make us what we are. Accordingly, ancestor-reverence holds an important place in the African belief system. . . . Egungun or egun is the Yoruba word used to describe those souls or intelligences who have moved beyond the physical body."

We can also remember the ancestor spirits in the sweet territory of silence or in contemplative practices. Ancestors can be present in our lives in a very real way. For example, if alcoholism has been a harmful family pattern, we have the opportunity to learn from the mistakes of our ancestors, and honor them by choosing not to extend that family pattern forward ourselves.

Sitting Meditation

In many spiritual traditions, *sitting meditation* is the universal posture used for accessing the human resource of wisdom. In silence, the sitter becomes the fair witness and suspends judgment of the process that is revealed.

Cross-culturally, sitting meditation is the learning or receptive posture that human beings assume to receive teaching or instruction of any kind. Besides instruction, many indigenous cultures also use this posture for silent prayer or careful observation of internal revelations.

The Teacher archetype asks that we become objective to our own processes. Sitting meditation teaches people how to wait, listen, and observe what is revealed. The *Tao Te Ching*, in Stephen Mitchell's translation, says, "True mastery can be gained by letting things go their own way. It can't be gained by interfering." Sitting meditation teaches us about the art of observation, where ideas and images are released as quickly as they are revealed. This is one practice of detachment. Other practices of detachment might include wilderness rope courses, river rafting trips, rock climbing, high diving, and fishing.

THE TEACHER'S CONNECTION TO NATURE

The principle Teacher of detachment in Nature is often *Grandmother Ocean*, who is the primary nature example of flexibility and resilience. For some native cultures, the direction of the *West* is the home of Grandmother Ocean and all the *water creatures*. The direction of the West, on the medicine wheel, is the place where many native peoples call forward the power of silence, wisdom, and ancestral guidance. The

West is associated with the season of *Fall,* the place of harvesting as well as letting go.

The water creatures and Grandmother Ocean reveal our capacities for abundant harvest and unlimited fluidity. We are a water planet. Indigenous cultures often hold water as sacred for its capacities to cleanse, nurture, heal, and purify. This direction reminds us that wisdom, like Grandmother Ocean, is always flexible and seldom rigid.

HOW THE UNCLAIMED TEACHER REVEALS ITSELF: THE SHADOW ASPECTS OF THE TEACHER ARCHETYPE, THE WOUNDED CHILD OF THE WEST

Patterns of Positionality, Judgment, and Control

Wisdom is the capacity to embrace the over-expressed and underdeveloped parts of who we are from the window of a fair witness. When we are able to value our self-worth as much as we listen to the self-critic, we begin to tap the resource of wisdom. We experience the shadow side of the Teacher archetype when we find ourselves in states of righteous *positionality, judgment, and control.* The Teacher embraces these states, but does not indulge in them.

The opposite of positionality is flexibility; the other side of judgment is objectivity and discernment; and the opposite of control is trust. Patterns of positionality, judgment, and control are generally fear-based and always reveal lack of trust. If, upon observation, we find that we over-express these patterns, we need to remember that we also carry an enormous gift of wisdom that is waiting to be fully engaged. People who have acute critical natures can utilize them in a constructive way. For example, people skilled at writing may write critical reviews, remembering to evaluate both what is workable and not workable in a project.

Universally, there are two sources of harm: *fear* and *ignorance*. Fear's major function is to alert us to something that may harm us so that we can heed the warning. Unfortunately, most of us feel fearful in a variety of situations that don't call for such protective measures. Fear's major effect is to constrict energy, which can harm us both mentally and physically and motivate us to fight or flee.

We do harm when we consciously ignore people or situations. We can also do unintentional harm in a state of "blissful ignorance." For example, we may casually say to a new acquaintance, "I really don't understand people who procrastinate"—unaware, however, that our new friend is a procrastinator and is struggling with that issue.

Confusion

Ignorance can sometimes be the source of *confusion*, which along with doubt is the shadow side of clarity. When we experience confusion, we should wait rather than act. If circumstances make it impossible not to act, we should seek pockets of clarity and act only in those areas.

Discernment is the ability to respect appropriate context, timing, and content. The discerning individual asks, "Is it wise to deliver this content at this time and in this place?" When we are caught in the shadow side of discernment, we find ourselves being blunt, inappropriate, and ignorant of context.

Attachments

The cycle which includes our coming and going
* Has no discernible beginning nor end;*
* Nobody has got this matter straight—*
Where we come from and where we go to.
* —The Rubáiyát of Omar Khayyam,* translated by Peter Avery and John Heath-Stubbs

Positionality reveals the presence of *attachments.* The Teacher archetype requires us to balance our capacities so that we are as detached as we are attached. When we find ourselves attached to outcome, our tendency is to control rather than trust. When we are attached to something, we often lose our objectivity about it, and thus lose our ability to do right by it. In a state of detachment, however, we carry the capacity to deeply care from an objective place. It is important to remember that wisdom is always flexible and seldom rigid. As we increase our capacities for flexibility, we increase our abilities to express our wisdom and to let go of our attachments.

For example, you may remember a time in your own life when you have stubbornly stuck to your position on a problem, but then been faced with options and perspectives you had not seen before. Suddenly, you see another—and better—solution. In this realization you moved from an attached position to a flexible place of wisdom.

Processes and Reminders: Important Practices to Develop the Inner Teacher

1. Spend at least fifteen minutes each day in sitting meditation. Record your experience in your journal or create a special meditation log.

Sitting Meditation

Accessing the Inner Teacher
Accessing the Quality of Wisdom

Purpose

The purpose of sitting meditation is to honor sacred time. This is a time set aside for introspection, contemplation, discovery, and honoring the sacred or divine.

Posture

Sit in a chair or on the floor with your eyes closed, and with your legs crossed or uncrossed. Both Eastern and Western practices incorporate the bent knee or praying posture, which is another posture used for sitting meditation.

Process

Within this sacred time and posture, you can ask for guidance or for ways to handle internal and external situations with wisdom.

Sitting meditation is an opportunity to transform the inner critic into the fair witness. It is also an opportunity to receive guidance and inner direction about handling your own life with wisdom.

Sitting meditation gives you the opportunity to move beyond the internal and external polarities, paradoxes, and oppositions that you are experiencing.

2. *Spend a portion of each day in solitude or in the sweet territory of silence for purposes of listening to your own knowing or wisdom. Set aside one full day a month to spend totally in silence.*

3. *Create some personal rituals to support you during transitions or times of loss.*

4. *Consciously make each day a focus for practicing wisdom. Ask yourself, How objective can I remain? Am I able to wait instead of act in times of confusion? Can I use discernment rather than judgment? Will I make decisions where I have clarity?*

5. *Daily practices that prepare us for the art of dying and handling the unfamiliar are situations where we say goodbye or when we go to sleep. In both of these daily practices, learn to trust and let go.*

6. *Spend some time honoring the richness of your roots and heritage.* Collect pictures of important ancestors. Use these as visual reminders of the "good, true, and beautiful" aspects of your heritage.

7. *On your birth date, each month, do something that you have never done before.* Incorporating this monthly practice into your life increases your capacity to consciously approach the unknown and unfamiliar at least twelve times during the year.

8. *During this year, what are the limiting patterns you choose to release from your nature so that you can more fully express who you are?*

The Earth is the center of the Universe
The house is the center of the earth
The family is the center of the house
The person is the center of the family.
—Basque Song

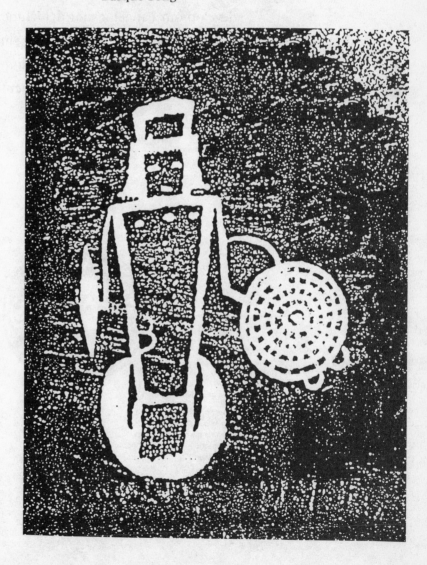

SUMMARY OF THE TEACHER ARCHETYPE

The Teacher archetype asks us to be open to outcome, but not attached to outcome. When we express the Teacher, we develop our capacities for detachment; we honor our heritage; we become flexible and fluid, like Grandmother Ocean; and we demonstrate wisdom and its components of clarity, objectivity, and discernment.

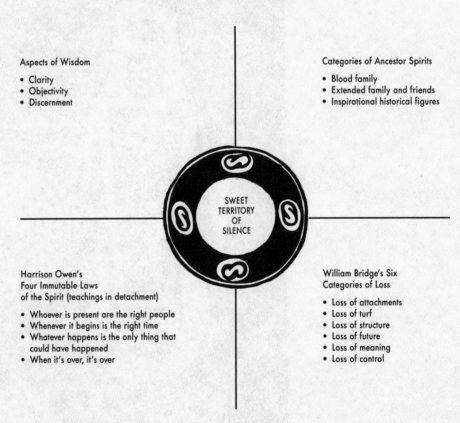

Aspects of Wisdom

- Clarity
- Objectivity
- Discernment

Categories of Ancestor Spirits

- Blood family
- Extended family and friends
- Inspirational historical figures

SWEET
TERRITORY
OF
SILENCE

Harrison Owen's
Four Immutable Laws
of the Spirit (teachings in detachment)

- Whoever is present are the right people
- Whenever it begins is the right time
- Whatever happens is the only thing that could have happened
- When it's over, it's over

William Bridge's Six
Categories of Loss

- Loss of attachments
- Loss of turf
- Loss of structure
- Loss of future
- Loss of meaning
- Loss of control

Questions

Think about your responses to the following questions. To develop the inner Teacher, ask and answer questions 4 and 7 daily.

1. Who have been the significant teachers in my life? Of these teachers, who were sources of inspiration and who were sources of challenge? What are the consistent qualities that I have been drawn to in these people, if any? What does this reveal about my own inner Teacher? Who have you been a teacher for, and who do you currently hold as a mentor?

2. Who are the trickster figures in my life who have taught me about flexibility and have revealed my patterns of positionality, judgment, and control? What "wake-up" calls have I experienced? How did I become aware of or "awaken" to limiting patterns that I have?

3. What attachments do I find in my personal life? In my professional life? In my spiritual life?

4. What is my tolerance level for silence and my capacity for being alone? Spend some time every day in silence. Enjoy some part of the day as your special alone time.

5. Who are the male ancestors that have both inspired or challenged me? Who are the female ancestor spirits that have both inspired and challenged me?

6. What is my capacity for waiting in times of confusion? What areas of my life carry confusion for me at this time?

7. *What current fears am I addressing? What am I consciously ignoring?*

8. *Of Harrison Owen's "four immutable laws of the spirit," which is the most difficult for me to accept or practice?*

9. *What life-negating family patterns am I consciously willing to break and no longer carry forward?*

10. *In my family background and heritage, what are the qualities that have been carried forward that I can identify as being "good, true, and beautiful?"*

11. *How have I handled loss in my life? Of the six categories of loss, which ones am I currently facing?*

≈≈≈≈≈≈

This is the Hour of Lead—
Remembered, if outlived,
As Freezing persons, recollect
*   the Snow—*
First—chill—then Stupor—
*   then the letting go—*
—Emily Dickinson, in
Johnson, *The Complete
Poems of Emily Dickinson.*

CONCLUSION

North, South, East, and West
the rich circle of my life
when my hoop joins yours.

—Richard Reiser

Walking the Four-Fold Way means opening to the universal archetypes of the Warrior, the Healer, the Visionary, and the Teacher, which lie within us waiting to express their wisdom in all of our actions and choices in the world. Most shamanic traditions believe that the Warrior's way is to know the right use of power, the Healer's way is to extend love, the Visionary's way is to express creativity and vision, and the Teacher's way is to model wisdom. Through the resource of power we are able to show up. Through the resource of love we are able to pay attention to what has heart and meaning. Through the resource of vision we are able to give voice to what we see, and through the resource of wisdom we are able to be open to all possibilities and unattached to outcome. William Blake may have been inspired by all four archetypes to write, "I in a fourfold vision see / And a fourfold vision is given me / Fourfold is my supreme delight . . . ." When we open to being powerful, loving, creative, and wise, we experience the world and ourselves as the many splendid things that we are.

Four Universal Meditation Postures

Types of Meditation Postures:

What Do They Reveal or Access for the Individual?

MEDITATION POSTURE	INHERENT RESOURCE ACCESSED IN POSTURE	INSPIRATIONAL QUOTE THAT APPLIES TO POSTURE
Standing Meditation	"Accessing the inner warrior" Resource: Power and Presence	"We convince by our presence." —Walt Whitman, *Leaves of Grass*
Lying Meditation	"Accessing the inner healer" Resource: Love	"Love, which created me, is what I am." —*A Course in Miracles*
Walking Meditation	"Accessing the inner visionary" Resource: Vision	"Vision quests are an age-old human practice for the grooming of one's spirit" —Brook Medicine Eagle, *Buffalo Woman*
Sitting Meditation	"Accessing the inner teacher" Resource: Wisdom	"What lies behind us and what lies before us are small matters compared to what lies within us." —Emerson (in Van Ekeren)

THE FOUR-FOLD WAY

THE WAY OF THE WARRIOR

THE WAY OF THE TEACHER

THE WAY OF THE VISIONARY

THE WAY OF THE HEALER

Direction: North
Element: Air
Creature: Winged Creatures
Human Resource: Power
Kind of Meditation: Standing
Way of Living: Right Action
Four-Fold Way: Show Up
Healing Salve: Dancing
Instrument: Rattle
Season: Winter

Direction: East
Element: Fire
Creature: Desert & No-Legged Creatures
Human Resource: Vision
Kind of Meditation: Walking
Way of Living: Right Placement
Four-Fold Way: Tell the Truth
Healing Salve: Singing
Instrument: Bell
Season: Summer

Direction: West
Element: Water
Creature: Water Creatures
Human Resource: Wisdom
Kind of Meditation: Sitting
Way of Living: Right Timing
Way of Living: Open to Outcome
Four-Fold Way: Silence
Healing Salve: Sticks, Bones
Instrument: Autumn

Direction: South
Element: Earth
Creature: 4-Legged Creatures
Human Resource: Love
Kind of Meditation: Lying
Way of Living: Right Speech
Four-Fold Way: Pay Attention
Healing Salve: Story-Telling
Instrument: Drum
Season: Spring

Cross-culturally, there are many different perspectives from the indigenous peoples of each continent regarding the directions and seasons. However, the majority view them as presented here.

Four Elements Medicine Wheel Prayer
Turtle Island West Coast
Ralph Metzner

O Great Spirit of the North,
Invisible Spirit of the Air,
And of the fresh, cool winds,
O vast and boundless Grandfather Sky,
Your living breath animates all life.
Yours is the power of clarity and strength,
Power to hear the inner sounds,
To sweep out the old patterns,
And to bring change and challenge,
The ecstasy of movement and the dance.

We pray that we may be aligned with you,
So that your power may flow through us,
And be expressed by us,
For the good of this planet,
And all living beings upon it.

O Great Spirit of the West,
Spirit of the Great Waters,
Of rain, rivers, lakes and springs.
O Grandmother Ocean,
Deep matrix, womb of all life,
Power of dissolve boundaries,
To release holdings,
Power to taste and to feel,
To cleanse and to heal,
Great blissful darkness of peace.

We pray that we may be aligned with you,
So that your powers may flow through us,
And be expressed by us,
For the good of this planet,
And all living beings upon it.

O Great Spirit of the East
Radiance of the rising Sun,
Spirit of new beginnings,
O Grandfather fire,
Great nuclear fire—of the Sun,
Power of live-energy, vital spark,
Power to see far, and to
Imagine with baldness,
Power to purify our senses
Our hearts and our minds.

We pray that we may be aligned with you,
So that your powers may flow through us,
And be expressed by us,
For the good of this planet Earth,
And all living beings upon it.

O Great Spirit of the South,
Protector of the fruitful land,
And of all green and growing things,
The nobel trees and grasses,
Grandmother Earth, Soul of Nature,
Great power of the receptive,
Of nurturance and endurance,
Power to grow and bring forth
Flowers of the field,
Fruits of the garden.

We pray that we may be aligned with you,
So that your powers may flow through us,
And be expressed by us,
For the good of this planet Earth,
And all living beings upon it.

APPENDICES

Hands that give also receive.

—Ecuadorian Proverb
(Feldman, *A World Treasury*)

The documents in these appendices reveal the international human rights to which all nations and human beings are entitled. They demonstrate the effort that is being made to retain and reclaim human rights worldwide. Peacemakers and earth stewards the world over have consistently given voice to what historian of religion Mircea Eliade states in *Shamanism* is an essential plea for the rediscovery of the spiritual history of humankind:

> Western man will not be able to live indefinitely cut off from an important part of himself, a part that is made up of fragments of a spiritual history, the significance and message of which he is incapable of deciphering. Sooner or later the dialogue with the "others"—the representatives of traditional Asiatic or "primitive" cultures—will have to be conducted, no longer in the empirical and utilitarian language of today (which is only capable of describing social, economic, political, medical, etc., circumstances) but in a cultural language capable of expressing human realities and spiritual values. Such a dialogue is inevitable; it is prescribed in the book of historical destiny, and it would be tragically naive to imagine that it can be pursued indefinitely on the mental level at which it takes place today.

By implementing our human rights, the human spirit has an opportunity to move toward respecting the richness of diversity which encourages the unfoldment of spiritual democracy.

APPENDIX A

The Spirit Shall Speak Through My Race

—Jose Vasconcelos, founder of modern education in Mexico
(Moody, *The Indigenous Voice*)

Eleanor Roosevelt's
International Bill of Human Rights*

Preamble: Universal Declaration of Human Rights

Whereas recognition of the inherent dignity and of the equal inalienable rights of all members of the human family is the foundation of freedom, justice and peace in the world,

Whereas disregard and contempt for human rights have resulted in barbarous acts which have outraged the conscience of mankind, and the advent of a world in which human beings shall enjoy freedom of speech and belief and freedom from fear and want has been proclaimed as the highest aspiration of the common people,

Whereas it is essential, if man is not to be compelled to have recourse, as a last resort, to rebellion against tyranny and oppression, that human rights should be protected by the rule of law,

Whereas it is essential to promote the development of friendly relations between nations,

Whereas the peoples of the United Nations have in the Charter reaffirmed their faith in fundamental human rights, in the

---

*Source: *International Bill of Human Rights* (Glen Ellen, CA: Entwhistle Books, 1981).

dignity and worth of the human person and in the equal rights of men and women and have determined to promote social progress and better standards of life in larger freedom,

Whereas Member States have pledged themselves to achieve, in co-operation with the United Nations, the promotion of universal respect for the observance of human rights and fundamental freedoms,

Whereas as common understanding of these rights and freedoms is of the greatest importance for the full realization of this pledge,

Now, therefore, THE GENERAL ASSEMBLY proclaims

This Universal Declaration of Human Rights as a common standard of achievement for all peoples and all nations, to the end that every individual and every organ of society, keeping this Declaration constantly in mind, shall strive by teaching and education to promote respect for these rights and freedoms and by progressive measures, national and international, to secure their universal and effective recognition and observance, both among the peoples of Member States themselves and among the peoples of territories under their jurisdiction.

Article 1

All human beings are born free and equal in dignity and rights. They are endowed with reason and conscience and should act towards one another in a spirit of brotherhood.

Article 2

Everyone is entitled to all the rights and freedoms set forth in this Declaration, without distinction of any kind, such as race, color, sex, language, religion, political or other opinion, national or social origin, property, birth or other status.

Furthermore, no distinction shall be made on the basis of the political, jurisdictional or international status of the country or territory to which a person belongs, whether it be independent, trust, non-self-governing or under any other limitation of sovereignty.

Article 3

Everyone has the right to life, liberty and security of person.

Article 4

No one shall be held in slavery or servitude; slavery and the slave trade shall be prohibited in all their forms.

Article 5

No one shall be subjected to torture or to cruel, inhuman or degrading treatment or punishment.

Article 6

Everyone has the right to recognition everywhere as a person before the law.

Article 7

All are equal before the law and are entitled without any discrimination to equal protection of the law. All are entitled to equal protection against any discrimination in violation of this Declaration and against any incitement to such discrimination.

Article 8

Everyone has the right to an effective remedy by the competent national tribunals for acts violating the fundamental rights granted him by the constitution or by law.

Article 9

No one shall be subjected to arbitrary arrest, detention or exile.

Article 10

Everyone is entitled in full equality to a fair and public hearing by an independent and impartial tribunal, in the determination of his rights and obligations and of any criminal charge against him.

Article 11

1. Everyone charged with a penal offense has the right to be presumed innocent until proved guilty according to law in a public trial at which he has had all the guarantees necessary for this defense.

2. No one shall be held guilty of any penal offense on account of any act or omission which did not constitute a penal offense, under national or international law, at the time when it was committed. Nor shall a heavier penalty be imposed than the one that was applicable at the time the penal offense was committed.

Article 12

No one shall be subjected to arbitrary interference with his privacy, family, home or correspondence, nor to attacks upon his honor and reputation. Everyone has the right to the protection of the law against such interference or attacks.

Article 13

1. Everyone has the right to freedom of movement and residence within the borders of each state.

2. Everyone has the right to leave any country, including his own, and to return to his country.

Article 14

1. Everyone has the right to seek and to enjoy in other countries asylum from persecution.

2. This right may not be invoked in the case of prosecutions genuinely arising from non-political crimes or from acts contrary to the purposes and principles of the United Nations.

Article 15

1. Everyone has the right to a nationality.

2. No one shall be arbitrarily deprived of his nationality nor denied the right to change his nationality.

Article 16

1. Men and women of full age, without any limitation due to race, nationality or religion, have the right to marry and to found a family. They are entitled to equal rights as to marriage, during marriage and at its dissolution.

2. Marriage shall be entered into only with the free and full consent of the intending spouses.

3. The family is the natural and fundamental group unit of society and is entitled to protection by society and the State.

Article 17

1. Everyone has the right to own property alone as well as in association with others.

2. No one shall be arbitrarily deprived of his property.

Article 18

Everyone has the right to freedom of thought, conscience and religion; this right includes freedom to change his religion or belief, and freedom, either alone or in community with others and in public or private, to manifest his religion or belief in teaching, practice, worship and observance.

Article 19

Everyone has the right to freedom of opinion and expression; this right includes freedom to hold opinions without interference and to seek, receive and impart information and ideas through any media and regardless of frontiers.

Article 20

1. Everyone has the right to freedom of peaceful assembly and association.

2. No one may be compelled to belong to an association.

Article 21

1. Everyone has the right to take part in the government of his country, directly or through freely chosen representatives.

2. Everyone has the right of equal access to public service in his country.

3. The will of the people shall be the basis of the authority of government; this will shall be expressed in periodic and genuine elections which shall be by universal and equal suffrage and shall be held by secret vote or by equivalent free voting procedures.

Article 22

Everyone, as a member of society, has the right to social security and is entitled to realization, through national effort and international co-operation and in accordance with the organization and resources of each State, of the economic, social and cultural rights indispensable for his dignity and the free development of his personality.

Article 23

1. Everyone has the right to work, to free choice of employment, to just and favorable conditions of work and to protection against unemployment.

2. Everyone, without any discrimination, has the right to equal pay for equal work.

3. Everyone who works has the right to just and favorable remuneration ensuring for himself and his family an existence worthy of human dignity, and supplemented, if necessary, by other means of social protection.

4. Everyone has the right to form and to join trade unions for the protection of his interests.

Article 24

Everyone has the right to rest and leisure, including reasonable limitation of working hours and periodic holidays with pay.

Article 25

1. Everyone has the right to a standard of living adequate for the health and well-being of himself and of his family, including food, clothing, housing and medical care and necessary social services, and the right to security in the event of unemployment, sickness, disability, widowhood, old age or other lack of livelihood in circumstances beyond his control.

2. Motherhood and childhood are entitled to special care and assistance. All children, whether born in or out of wedlock, shall enjoy the same social protection.

Article 26

1. Everyone has the right to education. Education shall be free, at least in the elementary and fundamental stages. Elementary education shall be compulsory. Technical and professional education shall be made generally available and higher education shall be equally accessible to all on the basis of merit.

2. Education shall be directed to the full development of the human personality and to the strengthening of respect for human rights and fundamental freedoms. It shall promote understanding, tolerance and friendship among all nations, racial or religious groups, and shall further the activities of the United Nations for the maintenance of peace.

3. Parents have a prior right to choose the kind of education that shall be given to their children.

Article 27

1. Everyone has the right freely to participate in the cultural life of the community, to enjoy the arts and to share in scientific advancement and its benefits.

2. Everyone has the right to the protection of the moral and material interests resulting from any scientific, literary or artistic production of which he is the author.

Article 28

Everyone is entitled to a social and international order in which the rights and freedoms set forth in this Declaration can be fully realized.

Article 29

1. Everyone has duties to the community in which alone the free and full development of his personality is possible.

2. In the exercise of his rights and freedoms, everyone shall be subject only to such limitations as are determined by law solely for the purpose of securing due recognition and respect for the rights and freedoms of others and of meeting the just requirements of morality, public order and the general welfare in a democratic society.

3. These rights and freedoms may in no case be exercised contrary to the purposes and principles of the United Nations.

Article 30

Nothing in this Declaration may be interpreted as implying for any State, group or person any right to engage in any activity or to perform any act aimed at the destruction of any of the rights and freedoms set forth herein.

APPENDIX B

What sets worlds in motion is the interplay of differences, their attractions and repulsions. Life is plurality, death is uniformity. By suppressing differences and peculiarities, by eliminating different civilizations and cultures, progress weakens life and favors death. The ideal of a single civilization for everyone implicit in the cult of progress and technique, impoverishes and mutilates us. Every view of the world that becomes extinct, every culture that disappears, diminishes a possibility of life!

—Octavio Paz, *The Labyrinth of Solitude*

World Council of Indigenous Peoples: Declaration of Principles*

1. All human rights of indigenous people must be respected. No form of discrimination against indigenous people shall be allowed.

2. All indigenous peoples have the right to self-determination. By virtue of this right they can freely determine their political, economic, social, religious and cultural development, in agreement with the principles stated in this declaration.

3. Every nation-state within which indigenous peoples live shall recognize the population, territory and institutions belonging to said peoples.

*Ratified by the Fourth General Assembly of the World Council of Indigenous Peoples, Panama, September 23–30, 1984.

4. The cultures of indigenous peoples are part of mankind's cultural patrimony.

5. The customs and usages of the indigenous peoples must be respected by the nation-states and recognized as a legitimate source of rights.

6. Indigenous peoples have the right to determine which person(s) or group(s) (are) included in its population.

7. All indigenous peoples have the right to determine the form, structure and jurisdiction of their own institutions.

8. The institutions of indigenous peoples like those of a nation-state must conform to internationally recognized human rights, both individual and collective.

9. Indigenous peoples and their individual members have the right to participate in the political life of the nation-state in which they are located.

10. Indigenous peoples have inalienable rights over their traditional lands and over the use of their natural resources. All lands and resources which have been usurped, or taken away without the free and knowledgeable consent of Indian peoples, shall be restored to them.

11. The rights of the indigenous peoples to their lands include: The soil, the sub-soil, coastal territorial waters in the interior and coastal economic zones all within the limits specified by international legislation.

12. All indigenous peoples have the right to freely use their natural wealth and resources in order to satisfy their needs and in agreement with principles 10 and 11 above.

13. No action or process shall be implemented which directly and/or indirectly would result in the destruction of land, air, water, glaciers, animal life, environment or natural resources without the free and well informed consent of the affected indigenous peoples.

14. Indigenous peoples will re-assume original rights over their material culture including archaeological zones, artifacts, designs and other artistic expressions.

15. All indigenous peoples have the right to be educated in their own language and to establish their own educational institutions.

Indian people's languages shall be respected by nation-states in all dealings between them on the basis of equality and non-discrimination.

16. All treaties reached through agreement between indigenous peoples and representatives of the nation-states will have total validity before national and international law.

17. Indigenous peoples have the right by virtue of their traditions, to freely travel across international boundaries, to conduct traditional activities and maintain family links.

18. Indigenous peoples and their designated authorities have the right to be consulted and to authorize the implementation of technological and scientific research conducted within their territories and the right to be informed about the results of such activities.

19. The aforementioned principles constitute the minimal rights to which indigenous peoples are entitled and must be complemented by all nation-states

APPENDIX C

Earth and heaven are in us.

—Mahatma Gandhi (Fox, *Original Blessing*)

Haudenosaunee, or Six Nations Iroquois Confederacy, Statement to the World—May 1979*

The Declaration was passed by the Six Nations Council of the Iroquois Confederacy on 27 April 1979 at the beginning of an environmental statement. The Council asked that the Declaration be reprinted to give "the widest circulation possible."

The Haudenosaunee, or Six Nations Iroquois Confederacy, is among the most ancient continuously operating governments in the world. Long before the arrival of the European peoples in North America, our peoples met in council to enact the principles of peaceful coexistence among nations and the recognition of the rights of peoples to a continued and uninterrupted existence. European people left our council fires and journeyed forth into the world to spread principles of justice and democracy which they learned from us and which have had profound effects upon the evolution of the Modern World.

The Spring marks the bicentennial of the Clinton-Sullivan Campaign, an invasion of our territories during the American Revolution which was intended to destroy the Haudenosaunee as a people. In their wake, the American armies left a "scorched

* Source: *Akwesasne Notes* (Spring 1979).

earth" path of frenzied destruction through our lands, leaving behind only ashes as they retreated from our territories. So fierce and malevolent was this action, that they ravaged cornfields, girdled fruit orchards, tortured and murdered Native women, and killed every living thing in their path.

It was the intention of the U.S. armies in 1779 that the Haudenosaunee be destroyed to the last man, woman and child. To that end, they waged war against our civilian populations and it is clear in our minds that they were interested not merely in our political and military defeat, but would rest at nothing short of the total annihilation of all that exists of the Haudenosaunee. We have survived that attack, and many more since then, but we are seriously alarmed at the events which have taken place over these two hundred years.

Brothers and Sisters: When the Europeans first invaded our lands, they found a world filled with the bountiful gifts of the Creation. Even the soldiers in General Sullivan's army were awed by the country they had entered, a land where a man could walk all day without seeing the sky, so rich and healthy was our forest. It was a land where the nearest branch of the trees stood fifty feet from the ground, and the trees were so great that three men holding hands could not embrace them. Sullivan's soldiers' words record what we would have told you —that the rivers ran so thick with fish that sometimes even wide streams a man could not see the bottom.

Everywhere the game was plentiful, and sometimes the birds darkened the sky like great clouds, so great were their numbers. Our country teemed with elk and deer, bear and moose, and we were a happy and prosperous people in those times.

Brothers and Sisters: Our Mother the Earth is growing old now. No longer does she support upon her breast the teeming herds of wildlife who once shared this place with us, and most of the great forest which is our home is gone today. The forests were butchered a century ago to make charcoal for the forges of the Industrial Revolution, most of the game was destroyed by sport hunters and farmers, most of the bird life has been destroyed by hunters and pesticides which are common this century. Many of the rivers flow thick with the effluence of great population centers throughout our country. We see that the "scorched earth" policy has not ended.

Brothers and Sisters: We are alarmed at the evidence that is before us. The smoke from the industrial centers in the Midwest and around the Great Lakes rises in a deadly cloud and returns to earth in the form of acid rains over the Adirondack Mountains, and the fish life cannot reproduce in the acid waters. In the high country of the Adirondack Mountains, the lakes are still, the fish are no more.

The people who plant the lands that we have occupied for thousands of years display no love for the life of this place. Each year they plant the same crops on the same land and they must then spray those crops with poisons to kill the insects which naturally infest their fields because they do not rotate crops or allow the land to rest. Their pesticides kill the bird life, and the runoff poisons the surface waters.

They must spray also the other plant life with herbicides, and each year the runoff from the fields carries these poisons into the watersheds of our country and into the waters of the world.

Brothers and Sisters: Our ancient homeland is spotted today with an array of chemical dumps. Along the Niagara River, dioxin, a particularly deadly substance, threatens the remaining life there and in the waters which flow from there. Forestry departments spray the surviving forests with powerful insecticides to encourage tourism by people seeking a few days or weeks away from the cities where the air hangs heavy with sulfur and carbon oxides. The insecticides kill the black flies, but also destroy much of the food chain for the bird, fish and animal life which also inhabit those regions.

The fish of the Great Lakes are laced with mercury from industrial plants, and fluoride from aluminum plants poisons the land and the people. Sewage from the population centers is mixed with PCBs and PBs in the watersheds of the Great Lakes and the Finger Lakes, and the waters are virtually nowhere safe for any living creature.

Brothers and Sisters: We are alarmed that a string of nuclear power plants is being built around our country and that at Three Mile Island in the southern portion of our ancient territories an "accident" has occurred which is a type of accident which could hasten the end of life in this place. We are dismayed that a nuclear waste dump at West Valley (N.Y.) upstream from one of our communities is releasing radioactive substances through our lands and into the watershed of Lake Erie. We are offended that the information about the nature of these plants is known only to the highest officials of the United States, leaving the people unarmed to defend themselves from such development and that the development of nuclear power is encouraged to continue.

We are seriously concerned for the well-being and continued survival of our brothers and sisters in the Southwest and Northwest who are exposed to uranium mining and its inherent dangers. The mining end is the dirtiest whether or not the machinery involved is dependable. Already vast amounts of low-level radioactive uranium tailings have been dumped in cities and used in building materials of dwellings and public buildings over a wide area of the Southwest. People have died, and many more can be expected to die.

Proponents of the Nuclear Fuel Cycle issue statement after statement to the people, urging that the nuclear reactors are fitted with safety devices so sophisticated that a meltdown is only the most remote of possibilities. Yet we observe that no machinery or other invention made by human hands was a permanent thing. Nothing humans ever built, not even the pyramids of Egypt, maintained their purpose indefinitely. The only universal truth applicable to human-made devices is that all of them fail in their turn. Nuclear reactors must also fall victim to that truth.

Brothers and Sisters: We cannot adequately express our feelings of horror and repulsion as we view the policies of industry and government in North America which threaten to destroy all life. Our forefathers predicted that the European Way of Life would bring a Spiritual imbalance to the world, that the Earth would grow old as a result of that imbalance. Now it is before all the world to see—that the life-producing forces are being reversed, and that the life-potential is leaving this land. Only a people whose minds are twisted beyond an ability to perceive truth could act in ways which will threaten the future generations of humanity.

Brothers and Sisters: We point out to you the Spiritual Path of Righteousness and Reason. We bring to your thoughts and minds that right-minded human beings seek to promote above all else the life of all things. We direct to your mind that peace is not merely the absence of war, but the constant effort to maintain harmonious existence between peoples, from individual to individual and between humans and the other beings of this planet. We point out to you that a Spiritual Consciousness is the Path to Survival of Humankind. We who walk about on Mother Earth occupy this place for only a short time. It is our duty as human beings to preserve the life that is here for the benefit of the generations yet unborn.

Brothers and Sisters: The Haudenosaunee are determined to take whatever actions we can to halt the destruction of Mother Earth. In our territories, we continue to carry out our function as spiritual caretakers of the land. In this role as caretakers we cannot, and will not, stand idly by while the future of the coming generations is being systematically destroyed. We recognize that the fight is a long one and that we cannot hope to win it alone. To win, to secure the future, we must join hands with like-minded people and create a strength through unity. We commemorate two hundred years of injustice and the destruction of the world with these words.

APPENDIX D

The Use of "Native American"*

The single most oppressive reality facing native peoples in North America has been the conscious and persistent unwillingness of United States people to recognize that native people are members of native nations. The argument that native people are not members of their own nations has long been used as a rationalization for the denial of native rights to land, water, and a way of life (and livelihood). In fact, the legal machineries of the United States and Canada have asserted repeatedly that native peoples either do not have status as nations or that their nations exist in a special relationship to the United States under which all rights to land and resources and even culture is less that those rights would be to any other people. There have even been standing policies in this hemisphere that assert that native people are not legally human beings because they do not possess a status as recognized nationalities, and therefore have no rights whatsoever.

Young people in the United States need to be sensitized also to the racist policies which have oppressed native people throughout the world, and encouraged to be able to identify those policies. The term Native American, in and of itself, is a seemingly harmless term, but it is used in a way that infers, however innocent its author, that native people are somehow

Our own preferences lead us to use terms such as "native people" rather than Native Americans because we feel that it is a more accurate term.

*Source: *Akwesasne Notes* (Late Spring 1977).

exactly the same as other hyphenated Americans (Chinese-Americans, Polish-Americans, etc.). That would not be objectionable, except that native peoples are in fact members of their respective nations, and the denial of their rights as distinct and separate nations with their own territories, sovereignty, cultures, and power over their own lives has been the basis of much racialist policy in the Western Hemisphere. Because of that history, our own preferences lead us to use terms such as "native people" rather than Native Americans because we feel that it is a more accurate term.

APPENDIX E

*Where I come from we say that rhythm is the soul of life,
because the whole universe revolves around rhythm, and when
we get out of rhythm, that's when we get into trouble.
For this reason the drum, next to the human voice, is our
most important instrument. It is special.*

—Babatunde Olatunji, Nigerian Drummer

The Journey of the Drum*

The Journey of the Drum

Why is it that the oral traditions of many indigenous cultures say that percussion in general and rhythmic drumming in particular facilitate communication with the spiritual world? Why does Nevill Drury, author of *The Elements of Shamanism*, write, "One thing never ceases to amaze me—that within an hour or so of drumming, ordinary city folk are able to tap extraordinary mythic realities that they have never dreamed."

I was a graduate student at the Institute of Transpersonal Psychology in the Fall of 1986 when I experienced my first "drum journey." The course was "Shamanism," a synthesis of universal principles of the wisdom of native cultures, taught by Angeles Arrien, a cross-cultural anthropologist and Basque

*Summarized by Melinda C. Maxfield, Ph.D., from her Doctoral Dissertation, *Effects of Rhythmic Drumming on EEG and Subjective Experience.* Presented to the faculty of the Institute of Transpersonal Psychology. Menlo Park, California, 1991.

folklore specialist. I was told to decide which world, upper or lower, I wished to visit. I decided to journey to the lower world in search of my power animal. I was to image an appropriate entry to the lower world. I was to ask any animal that appeared if it was my power animal. The power animal would reappear three or four times or sustain connection.

The journey for me was profound. I experienced vivid visual and somatic imagery, incorporating classic shamanic and archetypal themes. I was intrigued. There was nothing in my paradigm about "the way the world worked" that could account for my powerful images and emotional reactions. I mean, after all, I was in the middle of the suburb of Menlo Park, California, in a classroom with many other students, at three o'clock in the afternoon. How could this be? And what exactly is "shamanism," anyway?

Shamanism and the Shamanic Journey

Roger Walsh, in *The Spirit of Shamanism*, defines shamanism as "a family of traditions whose practitioners focus on voluntarily entering altered states of consciousness in which they experience themselves or their spirits traveling to other realms at will and interacting with other entities to serve their community."

Shamans are often referred to as "technicians of the sacred" and "masters of ecstasy." The shaman may journey to the upper world or the lower world. Images that are traditionally associated with an upper world journey include: climbing a mountain, tree, cliff, rainbow, ladder, etc.; ascending into the sky; flying and meeting a teacher or guide. The upper world journey may be particularly ecstatic. In the lower world journey, the shaman may experience images of entering into the earth through a cave, hollow tree stump, a water hole, a tunnel, or a tube and finding his or her power animal and animal allies. The lower world is traditionally a place of tests and challenges.

To accomplish the shamanic journey, the shaman enters into a specific type of altered state of consciousness which requires that he remain alert and aware. In this state, he or she is able to move at will between ordinary and non-ordinary reality. Michael Harner designates this pro-active state as a Shamanic State of Consciousness (SSC). There are various techniques for entering into the SSC, including sensory deprivation, fasting, fatigue, hyperventilation, dancing, singing or chanting, drumming, exposure to extremes of temperature, the use of hallucinogenic substances, and the set and setting dictated by the beliefs and ritualized ceremonies of the culture.

Journey Drumming

It was three years and many drum journeys later when I decided to train as a drummer. Several friends joined me, and we drummed on a regular basis. I had a wondering: Would it be possible to drum the *I Ching?* Yes, it was. The *I Ching*, or *Book of Changes*, is an ancient book of Chinese wisdom consisting of 64 hexagrams, each hexagram dealing with aspects and issues surrounding archetypal or universal energies. Each hexagram consists of six lines; these lines are either solid (——), or broken (——). Drumming patterns were derived from the hexagrams, the solid line representing one full beat and the broken line a half beat. We drummed the *I Ching*, writing music and taking people on journeys. The questions persisted: Why is it that the beating of the drum in this way can facilitate such powerful experiences? How could this tool be used in psychotherapy? Dream work? Healing?

From my own subjective experiences, I hypothesized that I was entering into an altered state of consciousness of some kind, related to, but not the same as, a meditative state. If this were so, then possibly it could be tested by measuring the electrical activity of the brain with an electroencephalogram machine (EEG). (Charles Tart defines an altered state of consciousness (ASC) as one in which a given individual "clearly feels a *qualitative* shift in his pattern of mental functioning, that is he feels not just a quantitative shift (more or less alert, more or less visual imagery, sharper or duller, etc.), but also that some quality or qualities of his mental processes are *different*.")

What would happen, I wondered, if I were to take some naive subjects, people who knew nothing about shamanism or drum journeys, into a biofeedback laboratory and have them experience the drumming? Could various drumming patterns be associated with specific brain wave activity? Would the subjective experience of percussion in general and rhythmic drumming in particular elicit images or sensations with a common theme? As I wrote my dissertation proposal, I decided that if it were not accepted, I would do the research anyway. My dissertation topic had "found me."

Brain Wave Frequency and EEG

To understand the results of this research, it is necessary to know some basic facts about EEG and brain wave frequencies. EEG is an instrument that produces a drawing of the various brain wave patterns. EEG waves are classified according to how many times a single wave occurs over a period of one second; this is known as wave frequency. Wave frequency is measured in terms of cycles per second, or Hertz (Hz), and by wave length. For example, a wave completing three cycles in one second is called a wave of 3 Hertz (Hz) or of 3 per second.

There are four major types of brain wave patterns, or *frequency bands:* delta, theta, alpha, and beta.

Delta (under 4 Hz) is the longest and slowest wave, i.e., this wave will repeat itself less than four times in one second. This wave is associated with sleep or unconsciousness.

Theta waves (4 Hz to 8 Hz) are usually associated with drowsy, near-unconscious states, such as the threshold period just before waking or sleeping. This rhythm has also been connected to states of reverie and hypnogogic or dream-like imagery. Often these images are startling or surprising. For many people, it is difficult to maintain consciousness during theta without some sort of training, such as meditation.

Alpha (8 Hz to 13 Hz) is associated with states of relaxation and general well-being. Alpha generally appears in the occipital region of the brain (the visual cortex) when the eyes are closed. Consciousness is alert but unfocused, or focused on the interior world.

Beta (over 13 Hz) is associated with active attention and focus on the exterior world, such as normal, everyday activities. Beta is also present during states of tension, anxiety, fear and alarm.

Research has confirmed that such spiritual practices as yoga and meditation produce changes in the electrical activity of the brain, leading to an increase in alpha and/or theta rhythms, and theta is found to be a characteristic brain wave pattern of long-term meditators. These meditators are able to keep their self-awareness intact, remaining alert in this "twilight state of consciousness."

Theory and Speculation

I was not the only one who had wondered about the connection between the drum and the spiritual realm. Other investigators, such as anthropologist R. Needham, had similar queries. He states that he finds "the common report, encountered again and again in ethnographical literature that a shaman beats a drum in order to establish contact with the spirits," and "All over the world it is found that percussion by any means whatever that will produce it, permits or accompanies communication with the other world." He asks, "How is one to make sense of the association between percussion and the spiritual world?" and states "The question seems not to have been asked . . . just why he beats a drum, and why this banging noise is essential if he is to communicate with spiritual powers."

This universally observed phenomena has been well documented but remains unexplained. There are, however, many theories and speculation: Are these effects caused by the elements of cultural conditioning, imagination, superstition? Is it the rhythm? Is it the monotony? Is there a physiological process involved? To date, there has been only a limited amount of scientific research on the physiological and neurophysiological effects of drumming. It was not until the pioneering work of Andrew Neher that acoustic stimulation in connection with the drum was tested. He supposedly confirmed the theory that rhythmic drumming can act as an auditory driving mechanism, bringing the brain into resonant frequency with an external auditory stimuli; however, his findings are thought by some to be critically flawed because he did not control for movement artifact.

Wolfgang Jilek, researching the drum beat frequencies contained in the ritual dances of the Salish Indians, found that the predominant frequency of the rhythmic drumming was four to seven cycles per second, the theta wave EEG frequency of the human brain. He hypothesized, as did Neher, that this frequency would be the most effective aid to entering an altered state of consciousness.

An immense body of ethnographic literature cites the many and varied uses of the drum within the secular and religious activities of many cultures. The specific uses of this instrument are as diverse as the cultures which employ them. These uses include: ritual and ceremony involving calendrical feasts, harvest and sowing, healing and sacrifice, celestial observations such as solstice, equinox, rites of passage (such as birth, death, initiation, marriage), processions, lunar rites, hunting, warfare, etc. Each culture has its own pattern of rhythms that are incorporated into ritual and ceremony.

The use of the drum in shamanic "journeying" is somewhat different from other uses, and practitioners claim that the drum is indispensable to their shamanic work. They say that they use it to enter into an altered state of consciousness and travel to other realms and realities, interacting with the spirit world for the benefit of their community. They say they ride their drum through the air; it is their "horse," their "rainbow-bridge" between the physical and spiritual worlds. Mircea Eliade, author of *Shamanism: Archaic Techniques of Ecstasy,* emphasizes that "the shamanic drum is distinguished from all other instruments of the 'magic of noise' precisely by the fact that it makes possible an ecstatic experience." Shamanic drumming, in the majority of cases, consists of a steady, monotonous beat of 3 to 4½ beats per second.

Into the Laboratory

My research was conducted with the biofeedback technology of MindCenter Corporation. This multi-user system is composed of four modules, each designed to block external source and light. The participants were able to lie down, the traditional journey posture. Each module contains a sound system.

From these modules, four cortical sites are monitored for theta, alpha, and beta brain wave activity. Bipolar (left and right) channels were recorded from scalp electrodes placed on the four cortical sites: left and right parietotemporal lobes and left and right parieto-central lobes.

Twelve participants were divided into three groups and monitored for EEG frequency response to three separate drumming tapes, which I and my drummers had recorded in a commercial sound studio. These tapes included: Shamanic Drumming, at approximately 4 to 4½ beats per second; *I Ching* Drumming, at approximately 3 to 4 beats per second; and Free Drumming, which incorporates no sustained rhythmic pattern. Four cortical sites, bilateral parietotemporal and parieto-central areas, were monitored for each participant during three sessions. No "journey" preparations were given; the participants were told to relax, to listen to the drumming tapes, and to try to be still, as any body movement was likely to create artifact.

At the conclusion of the sessions, each participant prepared a brief written account and was given a tape-recorded interview of his or her subjective experience. These subjective experiences were then categorized according to recurring themes and consensual topics.

Results

This research supports the theories that suggest that the use of the drum by indigenous cultures in ritual and ceremony *has specific neurophysiological effects and the ability to elicit temporary changes in brain wave activity,* and thereby facilitates imagery and possible entry into an ASC (altered state of consciousness), especially the SSC (shamanic state of consciousness).

A pattern that incorporates approximately 4 to 4½ beats per second is the most inducting for theta gain. Seven of the twelve participants showed varying degrees of increased theta during Shamanic Drumming.

Drumming in general, and rhythmic drumming in particular, often *induces imagery that is ceremonial and ritualistic in content and is an effective tool for entering into a non-ordinary or altered state of consciousness (ASC) even when it is extracted from cultural ritual, ceremony, and intent.* It is interesting to note that all twelve participants had some imagery, visual and/or somatic. For eight of these twelve, the images were vivid. This fact speaks to the power of the inducting force of the drumbeat in general, and the patterns of the Shamanic and *I Ching* Drumming in particular, to enhance imaging capabilities. It is hypothesized that the enhanced imagery capability is a direct result of theta frequency gain.

The pattern of the drumbeat as it relates to beats per second can be correlated with resulting temporary changes in brain wave frequency (cycles per second) and/or subjective experience, *provided the drumming pattern is sustained for at least 13-15 minutes.* In many instances, there is an accelerated shift in frequency increase or diminishment at minute 9, most notably for theta and alpha. According to field observations and subjective reports, the period of time required for most people to be affected/inducted by drumming appears to be thirteen to fifteen minutes. Generally, a rapid increase or diminishment of theta and/or alpha is seen to the fifteen minute point, with a gradual gain or diminishment on to the twenty minute point. This corresponds with the findings of meditation research as to the time required for optimum physiological response and, according to Angeles Arrien, to the oral teachings of some indigenous cultures concerning auditory stimulation.

The drumming also elicits subjective experiences and images with common themes. The first twelve categories are the common themes as synthesized from participants' verbal and written reports of their experiences in one or more sessions during the drumming. These include:

Loss of Time Continuum (LTC)

Seven of the twelve participants were aware of and stated that they had lost the time continuum, thus having no clear sense of the length of the drumming session.

Movement Sensations

This category includes the experience of feeling:

the body or parts of the body pulsating or expanding;

pressure on the body or parts of the body, especially the head, throat, and chest;

energy moving in waves through the body

sensations of flying, spiraling, dancing, running, etc.

Ten of the twelve participants experienced one or more of the "movement sensations" categories.

Energized

Nine of the twelve participants mentioned specifically that they became energized during and/or immediately after the drumming session.

Temperature Fluctuations (Cold/Hot)

Six of the twelve participants experienced sudden changes in temperature (e.g., chills, being flooded with warmth, sweating.)

Relaxed, Sharp/Clear

Five of the twelve participants noticed that they felt particularly relaxed, sharp, and clear. This was usually in lieu of emotions.

Discomfort

Five of the twelve participants mentioned specifically that they were in varying states of emotional or physical discomfort.

Out-of-Body Experiences (OBE)/Visitations

Three of the twelve participants stated that they had the experience of leaving the module or being visited by a presence or a person during the session. This category is differentiated from "Journey" in that no traditional shamanic imagery was present.

Images

Vivid Imagery: All twelve participants had some imagery. Eight of the twelve commented on experiencing vivid visual or sensate (somatic) images.

Natives: Nine of the twelve participants saw or sensed African, Tahitian, Eskimo, or Native American natives. These natives were usually participating in rituals and/or ceremonies involving dancing, singing or chanting, hunting, or drumming.

Animals/Landscapes: Seven of the twelve participants reported a wide range of animal and landscape imagery.

People: Nine of the twelve participants imaged childhood friends or important people from their past, "faceless" teachers, non-native drummers, unidentified faces, etc.

Journey: Five of the twelve participants' description of their experiences included classic shamanic journey imagery, such as: going into a hole or a cave; being shot through a tube or a tunnel spiraling up or down; being initiated; climbing an inverted tree; the appearance of power animals and helping allies.

Non-Ordinary or Altered States of Consciousness (ASC)

A majority of the participants, in one or more sessions, were conscious of the fact that there had been a qualitative shift in mental functioning, and the twelve themes as synthesized from the participants' oral and written reports may be correlated with Ludwig's delineations of features that tend to be characteristic of most ASCs. Eight of the twelve participants experienced at least one episode that was a journey, OBE, or a visitation; the data suggests that they achieved an altered state of consciousness (ASC). There was a total of thirteen such episodes for the thirty-five individual sessions.

Honoring All the Ways

It seems that there is validity for the ancient oral traditions that link the drumbeat with non-ordinary realities. How many other spiritual traditions hold tools for us to use for healing of mind, body and spirit? We can no longer afford to dismiss them as the product of an over-active imagination, superstition, or outright psychopathology and charlatanism.

Most indigenous cultures do not separate psychological from spiritual processes. Charles Tart emphasizes that "many primitive peoples . . . believe that almost every normal adult has the ability to go into a trance state and be possessed by a god; the adult who cannot do this is a psychological cripple."

Michael Harner states, "It is extremely difficult for an unprejudiced judgment to be made about the validity of the experiences in the contrasting state of consciousness. . . . The persons most prejudiced against a concept of nonordinary reality are those who have never experienced it."

It is now time to bridge the separate and often isolated disciplines of medicine, psychology, religion, anthropology, ethnomusicology, science, sociology, etc. If researchers in each of these areas continue to work in the vacuum of his or her own discipline, the exact nature of certain continually reported phenomena may never be found.

References

Arrien, A. (1989). Personal communication.

Achterberg, J. (1985). *Imagery In Healing: Shamanism and Modern Medicine.* Boston: Shambhala.

Drury, N. (1989). *Elements of Shamanism.* Longmead, Shaftesbury, Dorset: Element Books.

Eliade, M. (1964). *Shamanism: Archaic Techniques of Ecstasy.* (W. R. Trask, Trans.). Princeton: Princeton University Press.

Harner, M. J. (1980). *The Way of the Shaman: A Guide to Power and Healing.* San Francisco: Harper & Row.

Hart, M. (1990). *Drumming at the Edge of Magic.* New York: HarperCollins.

I Ching, Book of Changes. (3d. ed.). (1950) (R. W. Wilhelm, Trans.; rendered into English by C. F. Baynes). Princeton: Princeton University Press.(Bollingen Series XIX).

Jilek, W. G. (1982) Altered states of consciousness in North American Indian ceremonials. *Ethos* 10: 326–43.

Ludwig, A. C. (1968). Altered states of consciousness. In R. Prince (ed.). *Trance and Possession States* (pp. 69–95). Montreal: R. M. Bucke Memorial Society, McGill University.

Needham, R. (1979). Percussion and transition. In W. A. Lessa and E. Z. Vogt (eds.). *Reader in Comparative Religion* (pp. 311–17). New York: Harper & Row. (Reprinted from Man. 2. (1967, 606–14.)

Neher, A. (1961). Auditory driving observed with scalp electrodes in normal subjects. *EEG and Clinical Neurophysiology* 13: 449–51.

Neher, A. (1962). A physiological explanation of unusual behavior in ceremonies involving drums. *Human Biology* 34, no. 2 (May 1962): 151–60.

Tart, C. T. (ed.). (1972). *Altered States of Consciousness* (2d ed.). Garden City, NY: Anchor Books, Doubleday.

Walsh, R. (1990). *The Spirit of Shamanism*. Los Angeles: Jeremy P. Tarcher.

LISTING OF GRAPHICS

Cave art and ancient designs were selected as the art motif throughout the book, because every continent has cave art. These designs, which seem at once ancient and modern, serve to remind us all of humanity's deeper origins.

Introduction

Page x Lauburu. A Basque word/symbol for "four heads" (pre-Christian Basque cross). Photo: Jane English, taken in the Basque country.

Page 1 Lauburu. Drawing by Catalin Voda Dulfu.

Page 11 Cave painting. Inaouanrhat, Sahara Desert, Africa. Source: Douglas Mazonowicz, *Voices from the Stone Age: A Search for Cave and Canyon Art* (New York: Thomas Y. Crowell Company, 1974), 164.

The Way of the Warrior

Page 14 The Horned Goddess. Tassili, Aouarhet, central Sahara, North Africa. Source: Henri Lhote, *The Search for the Tassili Frescoes.* Translated from French by Alan Houghton Brodrick (New York: E. P. Dutton & Co, 1959), p. 89.

Page 15 Kneeling warrior. Source: Douglas Mazonowicz, *Voices from the Stone Age: A Search for Cave and Canyon Art* (New York: Thomas Y. Crowell Company, 1974), 59.

Page 30 Tree people. Rock paintings. Dona Clotilde Shelter, Albarracin region, Spain. Source: Mazonowicz, *Voices from the Stone Age*, 87.

Page 32 Chiltan postures. Left: Menhin, Colombia, ca. 1000 B.C. Right: Hirschlanden, Baden-Wuerttemberg, West Germany, Hallstatt culture, 600 B.C. Source: Felicitas D. Goodman, *Where the Spirit Rides the Wind* (Bloomington: Indiana University Press, 1990), 119, 157.

Page 37 Standing figure. Rock art, Petrified Forest National Park, Arizona. Source: Mazonowicz, *Voices from the Stone Age*, 176.

Page 39 Figure jumping fire. Rock painting. Sefar, Sahara Desert, North Africa. Source: Mazonowicz, *Voices from the Stone Age*, 159.

The Way of the Healer

Page 48 Reconstruction of honey-gathering scene. Rock painting. Araña, Spain. Source: Douglas Mazonowicz, *Voices from the Stone Age: A Search for Cave and Canyon Art* (New York: Thomas Y. Crowell, 1974), 92.

Page 49 Deer spirit. Source: Mazonowicz, *Voices from the Stone Age*, 139.

Page 51 Human figure in circle. Source: Jorge Enciso, *Designs from Pre-Columbian Mexico* (New York: Dover, 1971), 29.

Page 64 Left: Figure with leaves. Rock painting. Sefar, Tassili, Sahara Desert, North Africa. Right: Hand holding tree. Canyon art. Barrier Canyon, Utah. Source: Mazonowicz, *Voices from the Stone Age*, 136, 181.

Page 70 Reclining figure. Rock painting. Sefar, Tassili, Sahara Desert, North Africa. Source: Mazonowicz, *Voices from the Stone Age*, 137.

Page 72 Shaman figure canyon wall painting. Southeast Utah. Source: Mazonowicz, *Voices from the Stone Age*, 197.

The Way of the Visionary

Page 78 Painted figure. Canyon art. Lower Pecos River, Utah (from photo by Alan Gingritch). Source: Douglas Mazonowicz, *Voices from the Stone Age: A Search for Cave and Canyon Art* (New York: Thomas Y. Crowell, 1974), 179.

Page 79 Little eye. Eye Goddess. Almeria-Los Millares culture, Almizaraque settlement, Almeria, Spain; first half of third millennium B.C. Source: Marija Gimbutas, *The Language of the Goddess* (San Francisco: Harper & Row, 1990), 54.

Page 100 Walking figure. Rock art. Canada. Source: Mazonowicz, *Voices from the Stone Age*, 195.

Page 102 Eye Goddess. Almeria-Los Millares culture, Almiza-raque settlement, Almeria, Spain; first half of third millennium B.C. Source: Gimbutas, *The Language of the Goddess*, 54.

Page 105 African musical instrument. From traveling museum exhibition, "Sounding Forms: African Musical Instruments," 1989, sponsored by the American Federation of Arts, New York. Source: Collection at Musée National des Arts, Paris. Copyright © Photo R. M. N.

The Way of the Teacher

Page 108 Two sitting figures in circle. Cave painting. Inaouan-rhat, Sahara Desert, Africa. Source: Douglas Mazonowicz, *Voices from the Stone Age: A Search for Cave and Canyon Art* (New York: Thomas Y. Crowell, 1974), 164.

Page 109 Wave motif. Source: Joseph D'Addetta, *Treasury of Chinese Design Motifs* (New York: Dover, 1981), 51.

Page 114 Ancestor spirit figures. Barrier Canyon, Utah. Source: Mazonowicz, *Voices from the Stone Age*, 170.

Page 118 Percussion musician. Tassili, Africa. Source: Mazonowicz, *Voices from the Stone Age*, 130.

Page 123 Cross-legged sitting figure, rock painting. Sefar, Tassili, Sahara Desert, North Africa. Source: Mazonowicz, *Voices from the Stone Age*, 137.

Page 125 Figure holding shield. Engraved figure. Dinosaur National Monument, Colorado. Source: Mazonowicz, *Voices from the Stone Age*, 184.

Summary Charts

Pages 40, 74, 103, and 126 Summary Charts—Four Square Charts Center: Variant of the blue worm sign (Xonecuilli). Source: Jorge Enciso, *Designs from Pre-Columbian Mexico* (New York: Dover, 1971).

Pages 13, 47, 77, 107, and 132 Circular Charts. Designer: Constance King. Center: Four-fold designs that promote the turning of the great cycles of life are often composed of four circles or eggs around a common center, as on this Late Cucuteni bowl. Cucuteni B2 (Buznea near Peatra Neamt, Moldavia; 3700–3500 B.C.). Source: Marija Gimbutas, *The Language of the Goddess* (San Francisco: Harper & Row, 1990), 297.

Appendices

Pages 135–158 Stenciled hand images. Gargas, Aventignan, France. Source: Douglas Mazonowicz, *Voices from the Stone Age: A Search for Cave and Canyon Art* (New York: Thomas Y. Crowell, 1974), 21.

COPYRIGHT
ACKNOWLEDGMENTS

Paragon House, for citation from Allan Combs and Mark Holland, *Synchronicity: Science, Myth, and the Trickster* (New York: Paragon House, 1990).

Paulist Press, for citation from Brother David Steindl-Rast, *Gratefulness, the Heart of Prayer: An Approach to Life in Fullness* (New Jersey: Paulist Press, 1984).

Penguin Books Ltd., for verse 10 (p. 49) from *The Ruba'iyat of Omar Khayyam*, translated by Peter Avery and John Heath-Stubbs (Allen Lane, 1979). Translation copyright © 1979 by Peter Avery and John Heath-Stubbs.

Prentice Hall, for quotes from Glenn Van Ekeren, *The Speaker's Sourcebook: Quotes, Stories and Anecdotes for Every Occasion* (New Jersey: Prentice Hall, a Division of Simon & Schuster, 1988).

Richard Reiser, for his Haiku written at a workshop at the University of Humanistic Studies, San Diego, California.

Shaman's Drum, for complete article, "From the Editor," by Timothy White, *Shaman's Drum* 15 (Mid-Winter, 1989).

Shambhala Publications, Inc., for citations from *Woman As Healer* by Jeanne Achterberg, © 1990. Reprinted by arrangement with Shambhala Publications, Inc., 300 Massachusetts Ave., Boston, MA 02115. From *Zen Lessons: The Art of Leadership*, translated by Thomas Cleary, © 1989 by Thomas Cleary. Reprinted by arrangement with Shambhala Publications, Inc., 300 Massachusetts Ave., Boston, MA 02115.

Threshold Books, for citation from *Unseen Rain, Quatrains of Rumi*, translated by John Moyne and Coleman Barks, Putney, VT: Threshold Books, 1986.

University of Nebraska Press, for citation from John G. Niehardt, *Black Elk Speaks: Being the Life Story of a Holy Man of the Oglala Sioux as Told through John G. Niehardt (Flaming Rainbow)*. Lincoln: University of Nebraska Press, 1972, 5th cloth printing, 1989.

World Council of Indigenous Peoples, for the document from Douglas E. Sanders, "The Formation of the World Council of Indigenous Peoples," IWGIA, Document No. 29, 1977; and the document "World Council of Indigenous Peoples Declaration of Principles," Canada: WCIP, 555 King Edward Ave., 2nd Fl., Ottawa, ON, Canada K1N 6N5.

BIBLIOGRAPHY

Achterberg, Jeanne. *Imagery and Healing: Shamanism and Modern Medicine.* Boston: New Science Library, 1985.

———. *Woman as Healer.* Boston: Shambhala, 1990.

Alarcon, Francisco X. *Body in Flames.* Translated by Francisco Aragon. San Francisco: Chronicle Books, 1990.

Anderson, William. *Green Man: The Archetype of Our Oneness with the Earth.* San Francisco: Harper San Francisco, 1990.

Andrews, Valerie. *A Passion for This Earth: Exploring a New Partnership of Man, Woman and Nature.* San Francisco: Harper San Francisco, 1990.

Arrien, Angeles. *The Basque People.* A syllabus and integrated research outline. Berkeley: 1979.

———. *Cross-Cultural Research Outline.* San Francisco: 1987.

———. *Cross-Cultural Spiritual Perspectives.* Teaching Module. Menlo Park, CA: Institute of Transpersonal Psychology, External Degree Program, 1985.

———. *Cross-Cultural Values and Transpersonal Experience.* Teaching Module. Menlo Park, CA: Institute of Transpersonal Psychology, External Degree Program, 1987.

———. "Meditation: Four Portals to the Inner Life." *L.A. Resources* (August/September 1988).

———. *Signs of Life: The Five Universal Shapes and How to Use Them.* Sonoma, CA: Arcus Publishing Company, 1992.

Avery, Peter, and John Heath-Stubbs, trans. *The Ruba'iyat of Omar Khayyam.* London: Penguin Books, 1981.

Bach, Edward. *Heal Thyself: An Explanation of the Real Cause and Cure of Disease.* London: C. W. Daniel, 1974.

———. *The Twelve Healers and Other Remedies.* London: C. W. Daniel, 1975.

Bancroft-Hunt, Norman, and Werner Forman. *People of the Totem: The Indians of the Pacific Coast*. New York: Putnam, 1979.

Barks, Coleman, and John Moyne. *Open Secret*. Putney, VT: Threshold Books, 1984.

———. *Unseen Rain*. Putney, VT: Threshold Books, 1986.

Bateson, Gregory. *Steps to an Ecology of Mind*. New York: Ballantine, 1972.

Bayley, Harold. *The Lost Language of Symbolism*, vols. 1 and 2. New York: Carol Publishing Group, 1989.

Beck, Peggy V., and Anna L. Walters. *The Sacred: Ways of Knowledge, Sources of Life*. Tsaile (Navajo Nation), AZ: Navajo Community College Press, 1977, 1988.

Beck, Renee, and Sidney Barbara Metrick. *The Art of Ritual*. Berkeley: Celestial Arts, 1990.

Becker, James M., ed. *Schooling for a Global Age*. New York: McGraw, 1979.

Bennis, Warren. *On Becoming a Leader*. Reading, MA: Addison-Wesley, 1989.

Bernbaum, Edwin. *Sacred Mountains of the World*. San Francisco: Sierra Club Books, 1990.

Berry, Thomas. *The Dream of the Earth*. San Francisco, CA: Sierra Club Nature and Natural Philosophy Library, 1988.

Bible, King James version. Hamden, CT: Shoestring Press, 1968.

Bierhorst, John, ed. *The Sacred Path*. New York: William Morrow, 1983.

Bourguignon, Erika, ed. *Religion, Altered States of Consciousness, and Social Change*. Columbus: Ohio State Univ. Press, 1973.

Boyd, Doug. *Rolling Thunder: A Personal Exploration into the Secret Healing Power of an American Indian Medicine Man*. New York: Random House, 1974.

Bridges, William. *Surviving Corporate Transition*. New York: Doubleday, 1988.

———. *Transitions: Making Sense of Life's Changes*. Reading, MA: Addison-Wesley, 1980.

Burger, Julian. *The Gaia Atlas of First Peoples: A Future for the Indigenous World*. Garden City, NY: Anchor Books, Doubleday, 1990.

Cahill, Sedonia, and Joshua Halpern. *The Ceremonial Circle: Practice, Ritual, and Renewal for Personal and Community Healing.* San Francisco: Harper San Francisco, 1992.

Campbell, Joseph. *The Hero with a Thousand Faces.* Princeton: Bollingen Series, Princeton Univ. Press, 1949.

——. *The Masks of God.* 4 vols. NY: Viking Press, 1959, 1968.

——. *The Way of the Animal Powers.* Vol. 1. *Historical Atlas of World Mythology.* London: Summerfield Press, 1983.

Carroll, Lewis. *Alice's Adventures in Wonderland.* New York: Schocken Books, 1978.

——. *Through the Looking Glass & What Alice Found There.* Berkeley, CA: Univ. of California Press, 1983.

Catalfo, Phil. "Medicine Man." (An article on Bobby McFerrin.) *New Age Journal*, vol. 8, issue 2, March/April, 1991.

Chinen, Alan. *In the Ever After: Fairy Tales and the Second Half of Life.* Wilmette, IL: Chiron, 1989.

Clark, G., and S. Piggott. *Prehistoric Societies.* New York: Knopf, 1965.

Cleary, Thomas, trans. *Zen Lessons: The Art of Leadership.* Boston: Shambhala, 1989.

Combs, Allan, and Mark Holland. *Synchronicity: Science, Myth, and the Trickster.* New York: Paragon House, 1990.

Confucius. *Most Compelling Sayings by Confucius.* Translated by Leonard D. Lynall. *Most Meaningful Classics in World Culture Series.* Albuquerque, NM: American Classical College Press, 1983.

Conrad, Barnaby. *Famous Last Words.* Garden City, NY: Doubleday, 1961.

Costello, Peter. *The Magic Zoo.* New York: St. Martin, 1979.

A Course in Miracles. Tiburon, CA: Foundation for Inner Peace, 1975.

Davey, William G. *Intercultural Theory and Practice: A Case Method Approach.* Washington, DC: SIETAR International, 1981.

Davis, Courtney. *The Celtic Art Source Book.* London: Blandford Press, 1988.

Deal, Terrence E., and Allan A. Kennedy. *Corporate Cultures.* Reading, MA: Addison-Wesley, 1982.

de Unamuno, Miguel. *Tragic Sense of Life.* New York: Dover, 1954.

Dossey, Larry. *Recovering the Soul: A Scientific and Spiritual Search.* New York: Bantam Books/Doubleday, 1989.

_____. *Space, Time and Medicine.* Boulder, CO: Shambhala, 1982.

Drury, Nevill. *The Elements of Shamanism.* Longmead, Shaftesbury, Dorset, England: Element Books Limited, 1989.

Dundes, Alan. *Every Man His Way: Readings in Cultural Anthropology.* Englewood Cliffs, NJ: Prentice-Hall, 1986.

Dychtwald, Ken. *Body-Mind.* New York: Pantheon Books, 1977.

Eagle, Brook Medicine. *Buffalo Woman Comes Singing.* New York: Ballantine Books, 1991.

Eliade, M. *Shamanism: Archaic Techniques of Ecstasy.* Princeton, NJ: Princeton Univ. Press, 1964.

Elkin, A. P. *The Australian Aborigines.* Garden City, NY: Anchor/Doubleday, 1964.

Emerson, V. F. "Can Belief Systems influence Neurophysiology? Some Implications of Research on Meditation." *Newsletter Review. The R. M. Bucke Memorial Society* 5, 1972: 20–32.

Esar, Evan. *20,000 Quips and Quotes.* Garden City, NY: Doubleday, 1968.

Feher-Elston, Catherine. *Ravensong.* Flagstaff, AZ: Northland, 1991.

Feinstein, David. "Personal Mythologies a Paradigm for a Holistic Public Psychology." *American Journal of Orthopsychiatry* 49, no. 2 (April 1979): 198–217.

Feldman, Christina, and Jack Kornfield, ed. *Stories of the Spirit, Stories of the Heart: Parables of the Spiritual Path from Around the World.* San Francisco: Harper San Francisco, 1991.

Feldman, Reynold, and Cynthia A. Voelke. *A World Treasury of Folk Wisdom.* San Francisco: Harper San Francisco, 1992.

Feldman, Susan. *African Myths and Tales.* New York: Dell Publishing, 1963.

Ferguson, Alfred R., *et al.*, eds. *The Collected Works of Ralph Waldo Emerson.* Vol. 1, *Nature, Addresses and Lectures.* Cambridge, MA: Harvard Univ. Press, 1979.

Ferrucci, Piero. *Inevitable Grace.* Los Angeles: Jeremy Tarcher, 1990.

50 Anos De Pintura Vasca (1885–1935). Madrid: Museo Espanol de Arte Conteporaneo. October/November and December, 1971.

Fox, Matthew. *Original Blessing.* Santa Fe, NM: Bear & Co., 1983.

Franck, Frederick. *To Be Human Against All Odds.* Berkeley, CA: Asian Humanities Press, 1991.

Frank, Jerome D. *Persuasion and Healing: A Comparative Study of Psychotherapy.* Baltimore: Johns Hopkins Univ. Press, 1961.

Frazer, James G. *The Golden Bough: The Roots of Religion and Folklore.* New York: Avenel Books, 1981.

Fritz, Robert. *The Path of Least Resistance: Learning to Become a Creative Force in Your Life.* New York: A Fawcett Columbine Book/Ballantine Books, 1984, 1989.

Gallegos, Stephen Eligio. *Animals of the Four Windows: Integrating Thinking, Sensing, Feeling and Imagery.* Santa Fe, NM: Moon Bear Press, 1992.

———. *The Personal Totem Pole: Animal Imagery, the Chakras and Psychotherapy.* Santa Fe, NM: Moon Bear Press, 1987.

Geertz, C. *The Interpretations of Cultures.* New York: Basic Books, 1973.

Gimbutas, Marija. *The Language of the Goddess.* San Francisco: Harper & Row, 1990.

Giono, Jean. *The Goddesses and Gods of Old Europe: Myths and Cult Images.* Reprint. London: Thames and Hudson Ltd., (1974) 1989.

———. *The Man Who Planted Trees.* Reprint. Chelsea, VT: Chelsea Green Publishing, 1985; originally published 1954.

———. *Song of the World.* Reprint. San Francisco: North Point Press, 1980; originally published 1934.

Goldman, Daniel. *The Varieties of Meditative Experience.* NY: Dutton, 1977.

Goodman, Felicitas D. *Ecstasy, Ritual, and Alternate Reality: Religion in a Pluralistic World.* Bloomington: Indiana Univ. Press, 1988.

———. *How About Demons? Possession and Exorcism in the Modern World.* Bloomington: Indiana Univ. Press, 1988.

———. *Speaking in Tongues: A Cross-Cultural Study of Glossolalia.* Chicago: Univ. of Chicago Press, 1972.

———. *Where the Spirits Ride the Wind.* Bloomington: Indiana Univ. Press, 1990.

Graves, Robert. *New Larousse Encyclopedia of Mythology.* London and NY: Hamlyn, 1968; first ed. 1959.

Gray, Leslie. Personal conversation and co-facilitated workshop with Leslie Gray, San Francisco, CA, 1988.

Griffin, Susan. *Woman and Nature: The Roaring Inside Her.* New York: Harper & Row, 1978.

Grof, Christina, and Stanislav Grof, M.D. *The Stormy Search for the Self.* Los Angeles: Jeremy P. Tarcher, 1990.

Grof, S. *Realms of the Human Unconscious.* New York: Viking, 1975.

Grossinger, Richard. *Planet Medicine: From Stone Age Shamanism to Post-Industrial Healing.* Garden City, NY: Anchor Press/Double-day, 1980.

Hague, Michael. *Mother Goose.* New York: Henry Holt, 1984.

Halifax, Joan. *Shamanic Voices. A Survey of Visionary Narratives.* New York: E. P. Dutton, 1979.

———. *The Wounded Healer.* London: Thames and Hudson, 1982.

Hall, Edward T. *Beyond Cultures.* Garden City, NY: Anchor Press, 1976.

Harner, Michael. *The Jivaros: People of the Sacred Waterfalls.* Garden City, NY: Anchor/Doubleday, 1973.

———. *The Way of the Shaman.* New York: Bantam, 1982.

———. For drumming tapes by Michael Harner, write to: Foundation for Shamanic Studies, Box 670, Belden Station, Norwalk, CT, 06852. For *I Ching* drumming tapes, write to: c/o Maxfield, P. O. Box 2216, Saratoga, CA, 95707-0216.

Harnsberger, Caroline Thomas. *Everyone's Mark Twain.* New York: A. S. Barnes, 1972.

Harris, Philip R., and Robert T. Moran. *Managing Cultural Differences.* Houston: Gulf Publishing, 1978.

Hart, Mickey, with Jay Stevens. *Drumming at the Edge of Magic: A Journey into the Spirit of Percussion.* San Francisco: Harper San Francisco, 1990.

Heckler, Richard. *In Search of the Warrior Spirit.* Berkeley: North Atlantic Books, 1990.

Highwater, Jamake. *The Primal Mind: Vision and Reality in Indian America.* New York: New American Library, 1981.

Hillman, James. *Anima: An Anatomy of a Personified Notion.* Dallas: Spring Publications, 1985.

Hixon, Lee. *Coming Home.* NY: Anchor, 1978.

Hoopes, David S., ed. *Intercultural Soucebook: Cross-Cultural Training Methodologies.* La Grange Park, IL: Intercultural Network, 1979.

Hoppal, Mihaly, ed. *Shamanism in Eurasia.* 2 vols. Goettingen: Herodot, 1984.

Human Relations Area File (HRAF). Country Survey Series. Survey of World Cultures. HRAF Files, Inc. New Haven, CT: New Hraf Press/Yale Univ. Press, 1949–1990.

Huxley, Aldous. *Music at Night and Other Essays.* Salem, NH: Ayer, 1931, reprint series.

Ingerman, Sandra. *Soul Retrieval: Mending the Fragmented Self.* San Francisco: Harper San Francisco, 1991.

International Bibliography of Social and Cultural Anthropology. Paris: UNESCO, 1955.

International Bill of Human Rights. Glen Ellen, CA: Entwhistle Books, 1981.

Jain, Nemi C., ed. *International and Intercultural Communication Annual.* Vol. 5. Yarmouth, ME: Intercult PR, 1979.

Jimenez, Juan Ramon. *Three Hundred Poems 1930–1953.* Translated by Eloise Roach. Austin: Univ. of Texas Press, 1957.

Johnson, Robert. *Inner Work.* San Francisco: Harper & Row, 1986.

Johnson, Thomas H., ed. *The Complete Poems of Emily Dickinson.* Boston: Little Brown and Co., 1960, no. 1099.

Joy, Brugh. *Avalanche: Heretical Reflections on the Dark and the Light.* New York: Ballantine, 1990.

Kalweit, Holger. *Dreamtime and Inner Space: The World of the Shaman.* Boston and London: Shambhala, 1988.

Kanter, Rosabeth M. *The Change Masters: Innovation for Productivity in the American Corporation.* New York: Simon & Schuster, 1985.

Kazantzakis, Nikos. *The Odyssey: A Modern Sequel.* Translated by Kimon Friar. NY: Touchstone Book, Simon & Schuster, 1958.

King, Serge. "The Way of the Adventurer." *American Theosophist* (1985): 391–401.

Kinney, Jay. "Imagination and the Sacred with Kathleen Raine." *Gnosis* 23, Spring, 1992.

Krippner, Stanley, and David Feinstein. *Personal Mythology: The Psychology of Your Evolving Self.* Los Angeles: Jeremy P. Tarcher, 1988.

Lahr, Jane, and Lena Tabori. *Love: A Celebration in Art and Literature.* New York: Stewart, Tabori & Chang, 1982.

Larsen, Stephen. *The Shaman's Doorway: Opening Imagination to Power and Myth.* Barrytown, NY: Station Hill Press, 1988.

Laski, M. *Ecstasy: A Study of Some Secular and Religious Experiences.* New York: Greenwood Press, 1968.

Lawlor, Robert. *Voices of the First Day: Awakening in the Aboriginal Dreamtime.* Rochester, VT: Inner Traditions International, 1991.

Leach, Maria, and Jerome Fried, eds. *Standard Dictionary of Mythology, Folklore and Legends.* Ramsey, NJ: Funk & Wagnall, 1972.

Lehrman, Frederic. *The Sacred Landscape.* Berkeley: Celestial Arts Publishing, 1988.

Lewis, Hunter. *A Question of Values: Six Ways We Make the Personal Choices That Shape Our Lives.* San Francisco: Harper & Row, 1990.

Lhote, Henri. *The Search for the Tassili Frescoes.* Translated from French by Alan Houghton Brodrick. New York: E. P. Dutton & Co., 1959.

Lippitt, Gordon L., and David S. Hoopes. *Helping Across Cultures.* Washington, DC: International Consultants Foundation, 1978.

Machado, Antonio. *Times Alone: Selected Poems of Antonio Machado.* Translated by Robert Bly. Middletown, CT: Wesleyan Univ. Press, 1983.

Majno, Guido. *The Healing Hand: Man and Wound in the Ancient World.* Cambridge: Harvard Univ. Press, 1975.

Martin, Joanne, *et al.,* eds. *Organizational Symbolism.* Greenwich, CT: JAI Press, 1983.

————. *The Uniqueness Paradox in Organizational Stories.* Research paper #678. Palo Alto, CA: graduate school of business, Stanford Univ., 1983.

Maruyama, Magorah, and Arthur Harkins, eds. *Cultures Beyond Earth: The Role of Anthropology in Outer Space.* New York City, NY: Random House, 1975.

Matthiessen, Peter. *Indian Country.* New York: Viking Press, 1984.

Maxfield, Melinda C. *Effects of Rhythmic Drumming on EEG and Subjective Experience.* Doctoral dissertation. Menlo Park, CA: Institute of Transpersonal Psychology, 1991.

May, Rollo. *The Courage to Create.* New York: Norton, 1975.

Mazonowicz, Douglas. *Voices from the Stone Age: A Search for Cave and Canyon Art.* New York: Thomas Y. Crowell, 1974.

Mbiti, John S. *African Religions and Philosophy.* Garden City, NY: Anchor Books, 1970.

McGaa, Ed (Eagle Man). *Rainbow Tribe: Ordinary People Journeying on the Red Road.* San Francisco: Harper San Francisco, 1992.

———. *Mother Earth Spirituality.* San Francisco: Harper & Row, 1990.

Mead, Margaret. *Culture and Commitment. The New Relationships Between the Generations.* New York: Anchor Press/Doubleday, 1978.

Meier, C. A. *A Testament to the Wilderness: Ten Essays on an Address.* Santa Monica, CA: Lapis Press, 1985.

Metzner, Ralph. *Opening to the Inner Light.* Los Angeles: Jeremy P. Tarcher, 1986.

Miller, Alice. *Prisoners of Childhood.* New York: Basic, 1981.

Miller, Alice, Hildegarde Hannum, and Hunter Hannum. *Untouched Key: Tracing Childhood Trauma in Creativity and Destructiveness.* New York: Doubleday, 1990.

Milton, John. *English Minor Poems, Paradise Lost, Samson Agonistes, Areopagitica.* Chicago: Encyclopaedia Britannica, Great Books of the Western World Series, vol. 32, 1952.

Mindell, Arnold. *The Leader as Martial Artist.* San Francisco: Harper San Francisco, 1992.

Mitchell, Stephen. *Tao Te Ching. A New English Version.* New York: Harper & Row, 1988.

Monroe, Ruth H., and Robert L. Monroe. *Cross-Cultural Human Development.* Monterey, CA: Brooks/Cole, 1975.

Moody, Roger, ed. *The Indigenous Voice.* Vols. 1 and 2. London: Zed Press, 1988.

Morris, Desmond, Peter Collett, Peter Marsh, and Marie O'Shaughnessy. *Gestures.* Chelsea, MI: Scarborough House, 1979.

Mostakas, Clark. *Creativity and Conformity.* Princeton, NJ: Van Nostrand, 1967.

Munro, Eleanor. *Originals: American Women Artists.* New York: Simon & Schuster, 1979.

Neher, Andrew. "A Physiological Explanation of Unusual Behavior in Ceremonies Involving Drums." *Human Biology* 34 (May 1962): 151–60.

Nelson, R. K. *Make Prayers to the Raven: A Koyukon View of the Northern Forest*. Chicago: Univ. of Chicago Press, 1983.

Nerburn, Kent, and Louise Mengelkoch. *Native American Wisdom*. San Rafael, CA: New World Library, 1991.

Neruda, Pablo. *Five Decades: Poems (1925–1970)*. Bilingual ed. Translated by Ben Belitt. New York: Grove Press.

Nicholson, Irene. *Mexican and Central American Mythology*. London, New York, Sydney, Toronto: Paul Hamlyn, 1967.

Nicholson, Shirley. *Shamanism*. Wheaton, IL: The Theosophical Publishing House, 1987.

Owen, Harrison. *Leadership Is*. Potomac, MD: Abbott Publications, 1990.

Page, James K., Jr. *Rare Glimpse into the Evolving Way of the Hopi*. Washington, DC: Smithsonian Institute Press, November 1975. (Quote by Alonzo Quavehema.)

Paz, Octavio. *The Labyrinth of Solitude*. Translated by Lysander Kemp, Yara Milos, and Rachel P. Belash. New York: Grove Press, 1985.

Peter, Laurence J. *Peter's Quotations: Ideas for Our Time*. New York: William Morrow, 1977.

Peters, Larry G., "Using Shamanism for Personal Empowerment: An Interview with Leslie Gray," *ReVision*, vol. 13, no. 2 (1991).

Peters, Larry G., and Douglas Price-Williams. "A Phenomenological Overview of Trance." *Transcultural Psychiatric Research Review* 20 (1983): 5–39.

Radin, Paul. *The Trickster: A Study in American Indian Mythology*. New York: Schocken Books, 1972.

Ray, Dorothy Jean. *Eskimo Masks: Art and Ceremony*. Seattle, London: Univ. of Washington Press, 1967.

Rilke, Ranier Maria. *The Selected Poetry of Rainer Maria Rilke*. Edited and translated by Stephen Mitchell. New York: Vintage International, 1989.

Roberts, R., ed. *Four Psychologies Applied to Education*. Cambridge: Schenkman, 1974.

Rosenthal, Robert, ed. *Skill in Nonverbal Communication*. Weston, MA: Oelgeschlager, Gunn and Hain, 1979.

Roszak, T. *Person/Planet*. New York: Anchor/Doubleday, 1978.

Roth, Gabrielle, with John Loudon. *Maps to Ecstasy: Teachings of an Urban Shaman*. San Rafael, CA: New World Library, 1989.

Sandner, Donald. *Navaho Symbols of Healing*. New York & London: Harcourt, Brace & Jovanovich, 1979.

Sarton, May. *Journal of a Solitude*. Markham, Ontario: Penguin Books, Canada Ltd., 1973.

Schutz, William. *Profound Simplicity*. New York: Bantam, 1979.

———. *The Truth Option*. Berkeley: Ten Speed Press, 1984.

Segall, Marshall H., Donald T. Campbell, and Melville J. Herskovitz. *The Influence of Culture on Visual Perception*. Indianapolis: Bobbs-Merrill, 1966.

Severy, Merle, ed. *Greece and Rome: Builders of Our World*. Washington, DC: National Geographic Society, 1968.

Shaman's Drum: A Journal of Experiential Shamanism. P. O. Box 430, Willits, CA, 95490.

Shapiro, Barbara S. *Edgar Degas: The Reluctant Impressionist*. Boston: Exhibition catalog for the Museum of Fine Arts, Boston, 1974.

Smith, Elise C., and Louise F. Luce, eds. *Toward Internationalism: Readings in Cross-Cultural Communication*. New York: Harper & Row, 1979.

Smith, Houston. *Forgotten Truth*. New York: Harper & Row, 1976.

Snyder, Gary. Edited by Wm. Scott McLean. *The Real Work: Interviews and Talks (1964–1979)*. Toronto: A New Directions Book, 1980.

Spangler, David, and William Irwin Thompson. *Reimagination of the World: A Critique of the New Age, Science, and Popular Culture*. Santa Fe, NM: Bear and Company, 1991.

Starhawk. *Dreaming the Dark*. Boston: Beacon Press, 1982.

Steindl-Rast, Brother David. *Gratefulness, The Heart of Prayer*. Mahwah, NJ: Paulist Press, 1984.

Steiner, Rudolf. *Ancient Myths: Their Meaning and Connection with Evolution*. Toronto, Canada: Steiner Book Centre, 1971.

Stevens, Jose, and Lena S. Stevens. *Secrets of Shamanism: Tapping the Spirit Power within You*. New York: Avon, 1990.

Stewart, Edward C. *American Cultural Patterns: A Cross-Cultural Perspective*. Yarmouth, ME: Intercultural Press, 1972.

Storm, Hyemeyohsts. *Seven Arrows*. New York: Ballantine Books, 1972.

Storr, Anthony. *Solitude: A Return to the Self*. New York: Ballantine Books, 1988.

Sun Bear. *The Medicine Wheel: Earth Astrology*. New York: Prentice Hall Press, 1980.

Suzuki, Mitsu. *Temple Dusk: Zen Haiku*. Berkeley, CA: Parallax Press, 1992.

Teilhard de Chardin, Pierre. *The Phenomenon of Man*. New York: Harper & Row, 1959; reprint 1975.

Teish, Luisah. *Jambalaya*. San Francisco: Harper & Row, 1985.

Tiger, Lionel. *Optimism: The Biology of Hope*. New York: A Touchstone Book, Simon & Schuster, 1979.

Toffler, Alvin. *Future Shock*. New York: Bantam, 1971.

Triandis, Harry. *Handbook of Cross-Cultural Psychology*. 6 vols. Needham Heights, MA: Allyn & Bacon, Inc./Simon & Schuster, 1980–1981.

Tsunoda, Ryusaku, Theodore DeBarry, and Donald Keene. *Sources of Japanese Tradition*. New York: Columbia Univ. Press. 1958.

Turner, Victor. *The Ritual Process*. Chicago: Aldine, 1969.

Uhlein, Gabrielle. *Meditations with Hildegarde of Bingen*. Santa Fe, NM: Bear & Co., 1983.

Upanishads. Translated by Juan Mascaro (Classic Series). New York: Viking Penguin, 1965.

Van Ekeren, Glenn. *The Speaker's Sourcebook: Quotes, Stories and Anecdotes for Every Occasion*. New Jersey: Prentice Hall, 1988.

Van Gennep, Arnold. *Rites of Passage*. Chicago: Univ. of Chicago Press, 1961.

Vaughan, Frances. *Awakening Intuition*. New York: Doubleday, 1979.

———. *The Inward Arc: Healing and Wholeness in Psychotherapy and Spirituality*. Boston: New Science Library/Shambhala, 1986.

Veith, Ilza, trans. *The Yellow Emperor's Classic of Internal Medicine (Huang Ti Nei Ching Su Wen)*. New ed. Berkeley: Univ. of California Press, 1966.

von Franz, Marie-Louise. *Projection and Re-Collection in Jungian Psychology: Reflection of the Soul*. Translated by William H. Kennedy. Peru, IL: Open Court, 1985.

Wall, Steve, and Harvey Arden. *Wisdomkeepers: Meetings with Native American Spiritual Elders.* Hillsboro, OR: Beyond Words Publishing, 1990.

Walsh, R., and F. Vaughan. *Beyond Ego.* Los Angeles: Tarcher, 1980.

Walsh, Roger. *The Spirit of Shamanism.* Los Angeles: Jeremy P. Tarcher, 1990.

————. *Staying Alive: The Psychology of Human Survival.* Boston: Shambhala/New Science Library, 1984.

Warner, Mary Alice, and Dayna Beilenson, eds. *Women of Faith and Spirit: Their Word and Thoughts.* White Plains, NY: Peter Pauper Press, 1987.

Watts, Alan. *Beyond Theology.* Cleveland: Meridian, 1975.

Weatherhead, L. D. *Psychology, Religion, and Healing.* New York: Abingdon-Cokesbury Press, 1951.

Weil, M.D., Andrew. *Health and Healing.* Boston: Houghton Mifflin, 1983.

Whitman, Walt. *Complete Poetry and Selected Prose and Letters.* Edited by Emory Holloway. London: The Nonesuch Press, 1967.

————. *Leaves of Grass.* New York: Doubleday, 1954.

Wilber, Ken. *A Sociable God.* New York: McGraw-Hill, 1983.

————. *Up From Eden.* New York: Anchor/Doubleday, 1981.

Wilhelm, Richard. *The I Ching, or Book of Changes.* Translation rendered into English by Cary F. Baynes. Bollingen Series. Princeton: Princeton Univ. Press, 1977.

Williams, Margery. *The Velveteen Rabbit or How Toys Become Real.* New York: Doubleday & Co.

Wing, R. L. *The Tao of Power: Lao Tzu's Classic Guide to Leadership, Influence, and Excellence.* Garden City, NY: Dolphin Book/Doubleday, 1986.

Winkelman, Michael. "Trance States: A Theoretical Model and Cross-Cultural Analysis." *Ethos* 14 (1968):174–203.

Woods, Ralph, ed. *Treasury of Inspiration.* New York: Thomas Crowell, 1981.

Ywahoo, Dhyani. *Voices of Our Ancestors: Cherokee Teachings from the Wisdom Fire.* Boston: Shambhala, 1987.

INDEX

Achterberg, Jeanne, 52–53, 75
Acknowledgment: art of, 49; categories of, 74
Addictions, 65–68, 74
AH (sacred sound), 86
Aikido, 38
Alarcon, Francisco X, 105
Alice's Adventures in Wonderland (Carroll), 24
Alienation, 6
American Journal of Orthopsychiatry (Feinstein), 6
Ancestor spirits: calling on, 117–18; categories of, 126; connection through, 113–16; inspiration of our, 127
Animals. *See* Helping allies; Power animal
Archetypes: balance through expression of, 9–10; four principles of, 7–8; of Healer, 49, 74; of Teacher, 126; trickster, 110–11; of Visionary, 79, 84, 93, 103; of Warrior, 22, 40–45. *See also* Four-Fold Way
Art of acknowledgment, 49
Attachments, 122, 127
Authentic selves: described, 80–82; sources of inspiration and, 102
Authority issues, 34–35, 45
Avery, Peter, 122

Barrymore, Ethel, 99
Basque song, 125
Beck, Peggy, 55, 86
Bell work, 87
Birds, 32
Black Elk, Oglala Sioux, 7, 81
Black Elk Speaks (Neihardt), 81
Blackfeet, in Bierhorst, 73
Blake, William, 130
Blind spots, 99–100
Bly, Robert, 96
Body in Flames (Alarcon), 105
Bones: clicking of, 118
Book of Changes, 18, 117
Bridges, William, 4–5, 112, 126
Buffalo Woman (Brook Medicine Eagle), 131
Burger, Julian, 1

Carroll, Lewis, 21, 24
Chakras, 29
Challenges, 42
Change masters, 5–6
Change Masters, The (Kanter), 6
Chanting. *See* Songs
Ch'i, 22
Chiltan posture, 31, 39, 43
Clear mirrors, 95, 98
Cleary, Thomas, 20, 22
Clicking of sticks (or bones), 118

Coeur, 51
Combs, Allan, 110, 113
Communication: defining limits through, 17–18; with integrity, 83; judicious, 16–17; power of, 24; trust through, 17
Complete Poems of Emily Dickinson, The (Johnson), 128
Complete Poetry (Whitman), 31, 86
Conflict, 43
Confucius, 99
Confusion, 121–22, 127
Control, 120–21
Courage, 51
Courage to Create, The (May), 84
Course in Miracles, A, 131
Cradling work: described, 61–62; summary of, 74; to develop Inner Healer, 71

Dancing, 26–27, 41. *See also* Empowerment
"Dark Side, The" conference, 96
Death, 115, 124
Degas, Edgar, 55
Denial: false-self system, 93–94; patterns of, 81; self-abandonment mechanism, 94–95
Detachment: ancestor spirits, 113–16; four immutable laws of, 112, 126, 128; loss and ritual, 112–13; practices of, 119; theme of, 111–12. *See also* Loss
Dickinson, Emily, 128
al-Din Rumi, Jalal, 102
Directed prayer, 90
Direction symbolism: East, 77, 92–93; North, 32, 40; South, 47, 64; West, 107, 119
Discipline, 19–20
Dossey, Larry, 89
Dreaming the Dark (Starhawk), 5

Dreams, 21, 92
Drum, 57–58. *See also* Journey work
Drumming at the Edge of Magic (Hart), 57
Duncan, Isadora, 61
Dynamism (EE), 86

Eagle, Brook Medicine, 131
Eagle Man, Oglala Sioux, 80
East direction, 77, 92–93
Ecclesiastes 3:1-8, 127
Ecology, 3
Edgar Degas (Shapiro), 55
EE (sacred sound), 86
Egungun (or Egun), 118
Emerson, Ralph Waldo, 131
Empowerment: process of, 15; through dancing, 26–27, 41; through nature, 30–33; through power animals and allies, 28–29; through rattle work, 25–26; through standing posture and hand positions, 31–32; tools of the Healer, 54–62; tools listed, 40; tools of the Teacher, 116–19; tools of the Visionary, 85–92; tools of the Warrior, 25–29. *See also* Meditation
Eros, 59
Everyone's Mark Twain (Harnsberger), 117
Excellence, 67
Exercise, 39

Fall, 120
False-self system, 93–94
Famous Last Words (Conrad), 115
Father Sky: bridge between Mother Earth and, 50; symbolism of, 32

Fears, 115, 121, 128
Feinstein, David, 6
Feng shui, 25
First World, 4
Fixed perspectives, 99–100
Foundation for Shamanic Studies, 56
Four-chambered heart: checking condition of own, 72; concepts of healing, 52–53; described, 50–51; kinds of universal love, 52
Four-Fold Way: four principles of, 7–8; meaning of, 130; summary of the, 132. *See also* Archetypes
Four immutable laws of detachment, 112, 126, 128
Fourth World, 4
Four universal addictions: described, 65–68; fixated on what is not working, 68; to intensity, 66; to the need to know, 67–68; to perfection, 66–67
Four universal healing salves: cradling work, 61–62; described, 54–55; journey work and the drum, 56–58; lying meditation, 58–61; storytelling, 55–56
Four ways of seeing, 84
Four winds, 32
Franz, Maria von, 96

Gaia Atlas of First Peoples, The (Burger), 1
Gallegos, Stephen, 29
Gandhi, 22
Goethe, 115
Goodman, Felicitas D., 31
Grandmother Ocean, 119–20
Gratefulness, the Heart of Prayer (Steindl-Rast), 50

Gray, Leslie, 82
Gregorian chants, 87
Grief, 98. *See also* Projection

Hand positions, 31–32
Harm, 121
Harner, Michael, 56, 72
Hart, Mickey, 57
Healer: archetype of the, 49, 74; connection to nature, 62–64; developing the Inner, 69–72, 75–76; empowerment tools of the, 54–62; four-chambered heart of, 50–53; journey work of, 56–58; shadow aspects of, 65–68; "shape-shifter" as, 56; way of the, 8, 47–76
Healing: eight concepts of, 52–53, 68–69; principal of reciprocity and, 53–54
Heath-Stubbs, John, 122
Heckler, Richard, 20
Helping allies: accessing power through, 28–29; empower us in underworld, 61; honoring guidance of, 39
Hildegarde of Bingen, Saint, 63
Hill, Twainhart, 76
Hippocratic Oath, 47
Holland, Mark, 110, 113
Honor: defining, 15; extending, 44
Humanity, 6

I Ching, 18, 72, 117
Ignorance: harm through, 121; source of confusion, 121–22
Indian Country (Matthiessen), 30
Indigenous people: ancestral connections among, 114–16; culture of, 6; on directions and seasons,

Indigenous people *(continued)*
32, 40, 47, 77, 92–93; empowerment process, 15; expression of
archetypes, 9; Fourth World of,
4; importance of storytelling, 56;
inner and outer house connection, 3; Julian Burger describes,
1; paying attention to heart and
meaning, 49, 89; song and language expression, 86, 90; soul
retrieval work among, 25; sym-
bolism of trees, 31, 63; use of
reflective mirrors by, 95–96;
using power of movement, 39;
walking meditation by, 88–89
Indigenous Voice, The (Moody), 16
Indulgence, 81
Ingerman, Sandra, 25
Inner Healer, 69–72, 75–76. *See also*
Healer
Inner house, 3
Inner Teacher, 123–25, 127–28.
See also Teacher
Inner Visionary, 100–102, 104–5.
See also Visionary
Inner Warrior, 37–39, 41–45.
See also Warrior
In Search of the Warrior Spirit
(Heckler), 20
Insight, 84
Integration (AH), 86
Integrity, 83, 102
Intention: directed prayer and, 90
Interdependence principle, 5
Interface (between worlds), 4–5
Intuition, 84, 102
Isaiah 2:4, 19

*J*ambalaya (Teish), 118
James, William, 85
Job 12:8, 92
Joseph Nez Perce, Chief, 94

Journal of a Solitude (Sarton), 88, 90
Journey work: develop Inner
Healer through, 72; drum and,
56–58; images and memories
during, 59–60; lying meditation,
58–61; worlds visited during,
60–61
Joy, Brugh, 59
Judaic cantors, 87
Judgment, 120–21
Jung, Carl, 10, 91–92

*K*anter, Rosabeth Moss, 5–6
Ki, 22
Kimbala, Salon, 6
King, Martin Luther, Jr., 23

*L*abyrinth of Solitude, The (Paz),
53–54
Lao Tzu: on fear, 60; on returning
to source of being, 115; on true
mastery, 23, 107; on the Warrior's way, 28
Lawlor, Robert, 3
Leadership: developing, 42; inspiration of, 41–42; maintaining
balance in, 43–44; recognition of
your, 42; Warrior archetype
skills, 40; Zen teachings on, 20,
22
Leadership Is (Owen), 112
Leaves of Grass (Whitman), 23, 131
Logos, 59
Loss, 112–13, 126, 128. *See also*
Detachment
Love: arts of, 74; power of, 49; six
kinds of universal, 52, 74
Lying meditation: healing function
of, 58–61; posture, 131; to
develop Inner Healer, 69–71

McFerrin, Bobby, 89

McGaa, Ed, 80

Machado, Antonio, 48

Magnetism (OH), 86

Manuel, George, 4

Maps to Ecstasy (Roth), 27

Martin, Joanne, 55

Martyr, 65

Matthiessen, Peter, 30

Maxfield, Melinda, 58–59

May, Rollo, 84

Mead, Margaret, 54–55

Medicine: individuals with power of, 23; original, 21–22; power and, 20

"Medicine Man's Prayer" (*The Sacred Path*), 73

Medicine wheel: East direction on, 92–93; Four Elements Medicine Wheel Prayer, 133; South direction on, 64

Meditation: compared to prayer, 90; described, 87–88; four universal postures, 131; lying, 58–61, 69–71; sitting, 118–19, 123–24; standing, 27–28, 37–39, 43; walking, 88–89, 100–101. *See also* Empowerment

Meir, Golda, 82

Memory: significance of, 59

Metzner, Ralph, 133

Middle world, 61

Miller, Alice, 96

Milton, John, 116

Mirror, 95

Misunderstandings, 43

Moody, Roger, 16

Moon symbol, 32

Mother Earth: bell work and, 87; bridge between Father Sky and, 50

Mother Nature, 63–64

Mudras, 32

Music: bell work, 87; calling ancestor spirits with, 117–18; power songs, 85–86; sacred sounds of, 86; shamanic chanting, 87

Mythos, 59

Native American Wisdom (Nerburn and Mengelkoch): on common humanity of man, 39; on the Great Spirit, 7; on speaking the truth, 94; on Warrior archetype, 36

Nature: empowerment through, 30–33; Healer's connection to, 62–64; metaphors and symbols of, 32, 40, 92–93, 117; principle of reciprocity and, 53–54; symbolism of trees, 31, 63, 71, 117; Teacher's connection to, 119–20; Visionary's connection to, 92–93; Warrior's connection to, 29–33, 44

Neher, Andrew, 57–58

Nondirected prayer, 90

North direction, 32, 40

"Ode to My Father, Healing the Critic, An" (Hill), 76

OH (sacred sound), 86

Oikos, 3

Olatunji, Babatunde, 57–58

Open Secret (Rumi, trans. by Barks), 81

Original Blessing (Fox), 63

Original medicine: belief in, 21–22, 79–80; reawakening of our, 91

Outer house, 3

Owen, Harrison, 112, 126, 128

Page, James K., 26
Paradise Lost (Milton), 116
Path of Least Resistance, The (Fritz), 84
Pattern of denial, 81
Patterns of indulgence, 81
Patterns of invisibility, 35–36, 45
Paz, Octavio, 53
Perception, 84
Personal Totem Pole, The (Gallegos), 29
Physical exercise, 39
Position: lying posture, 58; power of, 24–25; universal meditation postures, 131
Positionality, 120–21
Power: of communication, 24; described, 20–21; losing, 43; of love, 49; of position, 24–25; of prayer, 55, 89–91; of presence, 23; singing songs of, 85–87, 101; through *ki* or *ch'i*, 22; universal, 22–23, 42
Power animal: described, 28–29; empower us in underworld, 61; honoring the guidance of, 39; identifying your, 44
"Power spots," 25
Prayers: compared to meditation, 90; consciously extending, 101; power of, 55, 89–91; types of, 90
Presence: power of, 23
Principle of reciprocity, 53–54
Projection: defining, 96; five stages of, 96–98
Proverbs 18:15, 117
Psyche, 59
Psychomythology: accessing the, 58; honoring our own, 59

Quavehema, Alonzo, 26

Rainbow Tribe (McGaa), 80
Rare Glimpse into the Evolving Way of the Hopi (Page), 26
Rather, Dan, 112
Rattle: developing Inner Warrior through, 38–39; soul retrieval work through, 26–27
Reality. *See* Middle world
Real Work, The (Snyder), 77
Rebellion, 33–34, 45
Recovering the Soul (Dossey), 89
Reflective mirrors, 95–96
Reiser, Richard, 129
Respect: defining, 15; extending, 44
Respicere, 15
Responsibility, 18–20
Rhythm: of chaos, 27; elemental, 27; flowing, 27; lyrical, 27; as soul of life, 57; staccato, 27; of stillness, 27. *See also* Drum
"Riding on the coattails," 35–36
Rites of Passage (Van Gennep), 6
Ritual: loss and, 112–13
Roosevelt, Eleanor, 22, 104
Roth, Gabrielle, 27
Rubáiyát of Omar Khayyam, The (trans. by Avery and Heath-Stubbs), 122
Rumi, 81–82

Sacred, The (Beck and Walters), 55, 86
Sacred Hoop: described, 80–81; empowerment tools and, 85; truth-telling and, 82
Sarton, May, 88, 90
Schutz, William, 82
Season symbolism: Fall, 120; Spring, 32, 47, 64; Summer, 77, 93; Winter, 32
Second World, 4
Self-abandonment, 94–95, 103

Self-esteem, 61–62, 71

Serra, Junípero, 115

Shadow aspects: authority issues as, 34–35; described, 10; of Healer, 65–68; of healing principles, 68–69; patterns of invisibility, 35–36; rebellion, 33–34; of Warrior, 40, 45; of Teacher, 120–22; of Visionary, 93–100. *See also* Archetypes

Shamanic traditions: ancestor spirits, 113–16; beliefs regarding archetypes, 130; bell work, 87; chanting, 87; cradling work, 61–62; functions of rattles, 26; journey work, 56–58; nature metaphors and symbols, 32, 40, 92–93; power animals, 28–29, 39, 44; power of archetypes in, 7; "power spots," 25; regarding self-abandonment, 94; rituals, 112–13; "shape-shifters," 56; significance of symbolism in, 60; on soul loss, 54; soul retrieval work in, 25–29; "spirit canoe," 58–59; use of standing posture/ rhythm of stillness, 28; trickster archetype, 110–11; on trust, 110–11; vision quests, 91–92. *See also* Meditation

"Shape-shifters," 56

Shapiro, Barbara, 55

Silence, 116–17, 127

Sitting Bull, Chief, 16–17

Sitting meditation: described, 118–19; developing Inner Teacher through, 123–24; posture, 131

Sky symbol, 32

Smoking mirrors, 95–96, 98

Snyder, Gary, 77

"Song of Myself" (Whitman), 31

Songs: power, 85–87, 101; as prayer, 90

Sonic driving, 57

Soul Retrieval (Ingerman), 25

Soul retrieval work: Healer and, 54–62; Warrior and, 25. *See also* Rattle

Sources of Japanese Tradition (Ryusaku Tsunoda), 16

South direction, 47, 64

Speaker's Sourcebook, The (Van Ekersen): Arabic proverb, 56; Dan Rather quoted, 112; Eleanor Roosevelt quoted, 104; Ethel Barrymore's statement, 99; Golda Meir quoted, 82; Lewis Carroll quoted, 21; meaning of leadership, 34; Rudolph Steiner quoted, 84; on singing, 85

Spells, 21

"Spirit canoe," 58–59

Spiritualism, 11

Split mirrors, 96, 98

Spring, 32, 47, 64

Standing meditation: function of, 27–28; posture, 131; process described, 37–39; working with process, 43

Standing posture, 31–32

Stars symbol, 32

Staying Alive (Walsh), 81

Stein, Gertrude, 84, 115

Steindl-Rast, Brother David, 50

Steiner, Rudolph, 84

Storytelling, 55–56

Stress-reduction techniques, 44, 58

Summer, 77, 93

Sun symbol, 32

Surviving Corporate Transition (Bridges), 112

Symbolism: directions and seasons, 32, 47, 77, 107; Mother Nature, 63–64; nature, 32, 40, 117; shamanic significance of, 60; of trees, 31, 63

Synchronicity: Science, Myth, and the Trickster (Combs and Holland), 110

Tai Chi, 38–39
Tao of Power, The (Wing's translation), 28
Tao Te Ching (Mitchell): on achieving true mastery, 119; on facing fear, 60; on setting priorities, 23; on source of being, 115; on true mastery, 107; on Warrior's way, 28
Teacher: connection to nature, 119–20; developing the Inner, 123–25, 127–28; empowerment tools of, 116–19; guiding principle of, 109; our significant, 127; qualities of wisdom, 109; shadow aspects of, 120–22; summary of archetype, 126; theme of detachment, 111–16; trust and, 110–11; way of the, 8, 109–28
Teish, Luisah, 118
Teresa, Mother, 49, 109
Third World, 4
Through the Looking Glass (Carroll), 21
Tibetan overtone sounds, 87
Time Alone (Machado), 48
Tragic Sense of Life (de Unamuno), 83, 89, 114
Trees: offering wound to, 71; quietude (rooted tree) and activity, 117; symbolism of, 31, 63
Trickster archetype: figures in our life, 127; theme of detachment and, 111; trust and, 110–11
Trust: judicious communication and, 16–17; nondirected prayer and, 90; way of the Teacher and, 110–11

Truth, 79, 82–83. *See also* Visionary
Truth Option, The (Schutz), 82
Tsunoda, Ruysaku, 16
Twain, Mark, 117

Unamuno, Miguel de, 83, 89, 114
Underworld, 61
Unexpected events, 39
Universal love, 52, 74
Universal powers, 22–23, 42
Upanishads, The, 111
Upper world, 60–61

VAK (Sanskrit goddess), 77
Van Gennep, Arnold, 6
Velveteen Rabbit, The (Williams), 90
Visionary: archetype of, 79, 84, 93, 103; authentic selves, 80–82; bell work, 87; connection to nature, 92–93; developing the Inner, 100–102, 104–5; empowerment tools of the, 85–92; four ways of seeing, 84; shadow aspects of, 93–100; truth principle of, 79; truth-telling, 79, 82–84; walking meditation, 88–89; way of the, 8, 77–105
Vision quests, 30, 91–92
Visions, 84
Voices of the First Day (Lawlor), 3

"Walkabouts," 89
Walking meditation: described, 88–89; developing Inner Visionary through, 100–101; posture, 131
Walsh, Roger, 81
Walters, Anna, 55, 86
Warrior: connection to nature, 29–33; developing the Inner, 37–39,

41–45; empowerment tools of, 25–29; extending honor and respect, 15–16; individual archetypes of, 22–23, 40–45; judicious communication by, 16–17; metaphors and symbols of, 32; responsibility and discipline of, 18–20; right use of power, 20–22; shadow aspects listed, 33–36, 40, 45; standing meditation by, 27–28; way of the, 7–8, 13–45

Water creatures, 119–20

Weil, Simone, 90

West direction, 107, 119

White Shield, Arikara Chief, 39

Whitman, Walt, 23, 31, 86, 131

Williams, Margery, 90

Wing, R. L., 28

"Winged ones," 32

Winter, 32

Wisdom: shadow side of, 67–68; teacher qualities of, 109, 120, 126

Woman as Healer (Achterberg), 52

Women of Faith (Duncan), 61

Women of Faith and Spirit (Warner and Beilenson), 55, 109

World order, 4

World Treasury of Folk Wisdom, A (Feldman): African-American proverb, 66; Cuban proverb, 110; on false-self, 93–94; Hawaiian proverb, 28; Maori proverb, 18; Russian proverb, 113; Spanish proverb, 80; Tibetan proverb, 63; Winnebago (Native American) proverb, 121; Yiddish proverb, 27

Wounded self, 71

Yoga, 32, 39

Yogic postures, 24

Yoruba Lucumi tradition, 118

Zen (Chan), 20

Zen Lessons: The Art of Leadership (Cleary), 20, 22